Bicycling MAGAZINE'S

CENTURY
TRAINING
PROGRAM

RODALE
LIVE YOUR WHOLE LIFE™

Every day our brands
connect with and inspire
millions of people to live
a life of the mind, body,
spirit — a whole life.

Bicycling MAGAZINE'S
CENTURY TRAINING PROGRAM

MARLA STREB

RODALE

To my father

© 2005 by Marla Streb

Printed in the United States of America

Rodale Inc. makes every effort to use acid-free ♾, recycled paper ♻.

Cover photograph by Stephen Alvarez/Getty Images

Interior photographs by Mitch Mandel (exercises only), David Smith, and Steve Sortino

Book design by Drew Frantzen

Library of Congress Cataloging-in-Publication Data

Streb, Marla.
    Bicycling magazine's century training program : 100 days to 100 miles / Marla Streb.
        p.   cm.
    Includes bibliographical references and index.
    ISBN-13 978–1–59486–184–0 paperback
    ISBN-10 1–59486–184–6 paperback
    1. Cycling—Training. I. Title.
  GV1048.S77 2006
  796.6—dc22   2005031319

Distributed to the trade by Holtzbrinck Publishers

2 4 6 8 10 9 7 5 3 1   paperback

LIVE YOUR WHOLE LIFE™

We inspire and enable people to improve their lives and the world around them

For more of our products visit **rodalestore.com** or call 800-848-4735

CONTENTS

I like plans. Complicated and detailed ones. Plans with contingencies and multiple backup scenarios. Timetables and bullet points and checklists. Multitasking and tight scheduling are always necessary. However, my plans allow for improvising and so much "initiative on the fly" that to those uniniti-ated to my system, it seems that I'm making it up as I go along.

This particular plan has a few major components. My brother, Dave, has a big part, and my boyfriend, Marc, has a supporting role. And the whole plan hinges around riding 100 miles in 1 day.

—Marla Streb

PROLOGUE

I nodded to myself. "If this southeast wind continues to massage the soft rolls of this building southern swell, in 36 hours on the other side of the Gulf Stream, I'll be on a bike ride from somewhere in Georgia to somewhere else in Georgia." Yup, just planning for a little bike ride.

"Shakedown Street" was shimmying from the stereo speakers through the salty air. I was lounging on the aft deck on a sailboat anchored in a shallow curve of a blue and white Bahamian Key, a glass of wine in one hand, my legs splayed out in a full hamstring stretch, the sun still yellow setting into the wide, shimmering glassy sea all around me.

A sunset Zinfandel had become a standard ritual during the past month. My fingers left greasy SPF imprints on the stem of the acrylic, unbreakable wine "glass." I rocked from side to side a little with the gentle actions of the water's swells. The wine splashed now and then on my thigh, but on a sailboat you learn quickly not to sweat the little things. Down below off to the starboard, where a real sailor would expect to find berths for crew, reclined three of my bikes: Two mountain bikes, one set up for urban assaults and the other for cross country, and one road bike were staggered side by side fork mounted onto quick-release skewers. They appeared ready to ride at a moment's whim if one could ignore the beach towels draped from the bar grips, the bikini tops dangling from the seat horns, and the snorkels, flippers, and scuba masks jostled in among the drivetrains.

The AAA road atlas of the American Southeast spread out on the nonskid surface of my boat's deck like a picnic blanket. Strewn on top of the road atlas were various sailing charts of the same regions. Interesting. If you look at a road map, there is plenty of detail. Usually, more information than you really ever need. Skinny lines demarcating interstates all the way down to unimproved dirt roads. Route numbers, mileage markers, rest areas, elevations, tolls, weigh stations, city, county, and state lines. Areas of Historical Importance. The names and boundaries of parks, forests, and wilderness areas. Train tracks, tunnels, bridges, and lots of other data. But road maps don't really provide much information about the waters. Rivers might be named, oceans or bays sometimes are colored blue, but their boundaries fall off the page an inch from the shoulder of the nearest road. The road maps point out how many feet high the mountains are but never reveal how many fathoms deep the bays are. The maps indicate the distances along the narrowest gray ribbon of road but not the miles of winding blue waterways. Funny.

Conversely, nautical charts have symbols for every navigation light, lines for every contour of depth, each submerged wreck, and even shades for good fishing grounds or poor anchoring areas. The nautical hieroglyphics whisper the story of the water's currents and tidal flows. The charts warn of hazards and encourage the sailor to stick to the safe passage routes. But the inland regions a scant inch from the waterways are blank. Bridges are drawn, but not the roads that lead to and from them. They just float magically over water unconnected to any surface road. The nautical chart displays the name of every rock that pokes through the water's surface, but provides not even the abbreviation of a city's name. Absent are multicolored lines thick and thin of the freeways, undivided highways, surface roads, and those roads left "unimproved." Where to ride a bike? Ashore of the water is the blank terra incognita of another era. Wouldn't be a surprise to see written in a flourishy hand, *"Thar be dragons here."*

The road maps and the sailing charts are of the same place but two different worlds.

"After we reach shore, I'll ride 100 miles and see how it goes," I said to myself. "It's only the width of five thumbnails," referring to the state of Georgia from border to border south to north.

Mountain biking is my specialty. On a singletrack you really don't need to know much about the trail you plan to ride. It's nice to know if the soil is muddy, rocky, or sandy, because tire choices can make all the difference between a morning of boundless joy and a day of frustration with your double-shot minipump. But you really don't have to know in advance where you'll be riding. No mountain biker ever writes on their sleeve a recipe of lefts and rights to follow on their ride. Most mountain bike rides are an end unto themselves: pointless by design. Getting lost in the woods is the understood goal. No one really rides trails to work or school. In that sense mountain biking isn't really a practical form of travel. Okay, in that sense it's like sailing.

Road riding is often predicated on reaching a destination such as the finish line or the next coffee shop. Road riding can be a very practical form of travel. All the great road rides are point to point. Sure, there are training loops, but the epic road rides begin and end in different places. The Tour de France, The Giro d'Italia, even the Race Across America. So you gotta know how to get from where you're starting to where you're ending.

The road map's lines were narrow, squiggly, and as flat as the elevation key every inch of the way. Hours of flat road riding every day up most of the East Coast for a couple of weeks wasn't really tingling my toes at the moment. I looked out toward the west, a splash of orange and red on top of the dark horizon's straight edge. I knew I'd feel better once I got back on the bike and rode along that flat edge for a while, and enacted my plan.

My plan. I called it a plan, but even Marc, my boyfriend, snickered at my plan's details. The gist of this part of my plan was that as soon as our sailboat brushed up against a wooden dock in the land of peaches, I'd hop off and hop on to my bike and ride north. A hundred miles or so later, I'd be waiting for Marc ashore of a quiet anchorage as he navigated our boat through the winding sloughs and across the sounds of the Intracoastal Waterway. There were some nuances to work out, but the idea was to hopscotch up the East Coast in that way right up to Baltimore, where my mom and dad still read their morning papers in the house in which I was born. During the previous 10 years, I had missed a lot of family occasions, birthdays, and tooth fairy visitations because I was chasing a career as a pro cyclist. So my plan was an extended visit back home with my family. This ride up the East Coast should take a few weeks, I figured. I'd be rolling along river roads, over wooden bridges, past lighthouses, swamps, and some strip malls to be sure, but through some country whose topography was essentially unchanged since European settlement, because its contours were savaged by each hurricane season. Flat. Yes. Not my favorite kind of riding, but I can get used to it, and there were still plenty of opportunities to get lost, I noticed as I looked over the spread of papers scattered on the deck. On the road map in the bluish green of the Intracoastal Waterway's edges I had drawn at intervals of 100 miles a crude pencil version of an anchor. This plan was a test run. A beta rollout. On the sailing charts in water at least 10 feet deep (our boat's keel draws 6), I had drawn a smiley face at the corresponding 100-mile intervals. That's where Marc would anchor and then row ashore and pick me up, and then make me dinner.

One hundred is a nice round number. It's metric and decimal. Familiar and easy to work with. A Century doesn't start out like that, though. Seems too big and too far away. You begin with time clicked off in increments of 60 seconds at first. Then minutes into hours stretching toward the horizon until you start measuring time in decades: the units of a Century.

I'll be starting my fourth decade pretty soon.

Similarly, distance sets out in units of 12, from inch to foot, foot factored to fathom or furlong and so on. But even here in America where the metric system exists only in a shadowy parallel world unrealized by us most of the time, we do recognize that miles measured out to 100 reaches a kind of perfection. When you're riding a bike for 100 miles, a Century Ride, the time and distance really do converge. When you're riding your bike for 100 miles, an intimacy develops with your cycle computer. Your miles per hour become paramount. Whether the average speed is 10 or 20 miles an hour, you soon realize that the slower you go the further you still have to go. And, if you can kick it up a notch, and hold it there, you just lopped off a huge part of the remaining distance.

The water had swallowed all but the last curves of the sun's most brilliant rays. I began to fold up the papers while there was still some light. In the morning we would be hauling up the anchor even before the sun rose. The paper folds of the maps and charts slipped into the canvas, rubber-lined pouch of an old bike messenger bag, which long ago had lost its shoulder straps.

The last swallow of *Zin* I swirled in my plastic stemware. I was trying to time it so that I could savor the last sip while enjoying the momentary afterglow of a sun already on its way to becoming part of tomorrow. This upcoming ride along the East Coast is a practice test. I hope in a year or two to sail and ride my bike around the world. Easier to imagine it will actually happen if I can reduce its scope to sailing 100 miles a day, and then riding my bike 100 miles a day as well. Sail 2 or 3 days, get off and ride for 2 or 3 days, and hopscotch like that a little bit at a time, a hundred miles at a clip all the way around the world. But for me, riding 4 or 5 hours on the road day after day will be an experience apart from the mountain biking on dirt that

I've so enjoyed for the last 10 years. Learning to end up at the finish of the day where I'm supposed to be will be a new challenge. When I get to Baltimore, I plan to break in my brother Dave; get him on a training program to build him up to the point where a Century Ride can be a regular event. I'll start with Dave; he's already a weekend roadie. And then my other brothers, Chris and John. Riding with my brothers is the best way of spending some time with them. During my big trip around the world, I hope to enjoy this revolving crew of pretty decent riding partners while Marc sails the boat, prepares us breakfast and dinner, ferries us ashore and back on our dingy, and deals with most of the practical wrinkles of my plan. I steadied myself by holding on to the wooden spokes of the boat's wheel and stood up. I lit and hung the kerosene anchor lamp from the rigging and then climbed through the narrow passageway and down the three well-worn steps below to the bed where Marc was already snoring softly.

Bicycling MAGAZINE'S

CENTURY TRAINING PROGRAM

INTRODUCTION

The concept of a Century Ride is not easily arrived at. That one can get so much out of a single day's challenge is a testament to self-satisfaction. Elite cyclists do Centuries all the time without much thought about it . . . just a long slow day, some hill climbs, or an afternoon of time spent with friends. For enthusiasts, a Century may be a lifetime first. But riding a bicycle 100 miles has universal appeal.

What Is a Century Ride?

For those who haven't ridden one, a Century Ride is a 100-mile bike ride. For those who have ridden one, a Century Ride can be much more.

A Century Ride is unlike the marathon, whose 26 miles is stepped off in commemoration of an actual heroic run thousands of years ago in Greece.

The first Century Ride has no pinpoint in time. The great age of the bicycle began somewhere in the soot of the second half of the 19th century. Comparatively more capital was invested in bicycle technology then, than just recently in the Internet boom, and similarly as many fortunes were won as lost. More patents were filed for bicycles at that time than have been filed to date for space travel. The relative per capita investment for paved roads for the use of bicycles exceeded the original funding for the federal interstate highway system. Some time during this great heyday of the two-wheeler, somewhere someone first said, "Hey, let's go for a 100-mile bike ride." I'm sure that his friends just stared at him and thought, "Why?"

The first proposed Century Ride was a challenge to be enjoined, not necessarily met. In that age, the average locomotive huffing and puffing the 100-mile distance from New York's Grand Central Station to Hartford, Connecticut, took about 4 hours and required the infrastructure and rolling stock of a whole railroad line, the investment of stockholders worth millions, and the labor of hundreds of employees. So, the thought of propelling oneself on a bicycle the same distance in a comparable amount of time requiring only the purchase price of a *safety bicycle* and some healthy exertion was beyond most people's credulity.

Cyclists called themselves wheelmen. Horse and buggy drivers and pedestrians shouted out other more colorful names for cyclists. Although women scandalously did ride bikes, there were no "wheelwomen" to speak of. The wheelmen were the extreme athletes of the time.

Since the bulk of commercial traffic was borne on canals like the Erie, or on the spider web of freight and passenger rails, the development and maintenance of roads was largely neglected. A town's Main Street always looked nice, paved as it might be with brick or cobblestone, but a few miles from the center of metropolitan cities the paved roads would typically give way to dirt and gravel. Ruts from horse and wagon, nonexistent drainage, and herds of cows or sheep were just some of the conditions that cyclists would have had to contend with during a

Century Ride. It's ironic that today cyclists must fight with cars to share the roads that cyclists originally lobbied the government to pave.

In fact, *The Vehicle Code* was developed in response to the popularity of bicycles on city streets. Prior to bikes, there was little need for the codification of speed limits, turn signals, the use of horns, U-turns, how to overtake a slower vehicle, etc. The publication of the first *Rules of the Road* was an attempt by the general populace to reign in the free-wheeling wheelmen whose safety bicycles could reach speeds in excess of 25 miles an hour and whose silent approach offered no warning to pedestrians. Horses bucked, pedestrians were taken aback, and streetcar operators were on edge whenever bicycles swerved onto the street. As a solution, various schemes were tried by different cities and towns. Some towns prohibited bicycles from the streets altogether and instead relegated them to parks. Other places denied the paths and promenades of parks to bikes and maintained that they could only be lawfully ridden on streets. Their hours of operation were regulated to daylight only; some places allowed their use only on weekends.

Due to the burden of complying with the growing body of regulation and in response to unfavorable public opinion, many bike clubs disbanded. Those clubs who endured and those riders who persevered often did so by ceasing to ride in cities or towns, but rather by riding away from these urban cores out into the countryside where there were fewer pedestrians, less dense horse traffic, and nonexistent bicycle regulations.

Today, an elite cyclist views a Century Ride in a manner different from the perspective of a recreational rider. Everybody can benefit from a Century Ride, whether it's a weekly event for some or a lifetime achievement for others. Some of these benefits are an increase in basic health and fitness, the development of mental strength, or the setting and achieving of a particular goal. And this can be a stimulus to strive for other goals which otherwise might have seemed unobtainable and an opportunity for a lifestyle change that can be lifelong.

As a professional cyclist, I've ridden Centuries early in the training season in order to build a base. I haven't gone on many formal

Century Rides, but have certainly ridden many informal and private ones. Other mountain bikers, and especially gravity racers whose events rarely last more than a few minutes, might disagree with me, but I am convinced that a large part of my success is due to the long hours I've logged on my road bike. Over the years I've won numerous NORBA national downhills, a World Cup and an X Game gold, and a Singlespeed World Championship. The base level of fitness that these Century Rides have provided me also contributed to many respectable finishes in cyclocross and 24-hour races.

Usually, after the winter holidays I look at my bike in a new light, asking what I expect out of it and from myself during the upcoming race season. The questions themselves and certainly the answers don't come easily. I've found that the best thing for me to do is go on long road rides and wait for the questions and answers to come of their own accord.

On these road rides during the late winter midmornings, I work on my form. For the first few weeks on smooth country roads in Marin County or on the Central Coast, I ride alone and concentrate on perfecting the smooth circle of my pedal stroke. I have been fortunate that most years I've been able to take care of any problems discovered during these long rides by some minor adjustments to my bike. Maybe a small equipment change. Some years, I've discovered that there was an injury that didn't heal correctly or fully, and some rehab was required. Much better to take care of all that now, the ice, the compression wraps, targeted massage, or some particular exercises before I begin to stress my body with the heavy training required for the upcoming season.

I usually don't pay attention to the mileage during these rides. I'm happy to gauge my progress by the amount of time ridden. I try to throw in some big efforts during hill climbs. I take into account the negative effects of a headwind, or a double flat, and I don't allow myself to become too upset if I'm not having a good ride. My investment in an iPod has really paid off in this regard. David Byrne and Jerry Garcia always urge me on to go for the larger loop.

Even as a pro cyclist, during the early season, I have to sneak up on a Century Ride. Riding 100 miles is a lot to ask not only of your butt, but your brain as well. One hundred miles can be a long time in the saddle, but an even longer time in your helmet. I find I can tune out the pain in my arms or legs. I can ride at an easy pace so that my lungs won't blow up. I can squirm around enough on the saddle and stand on my pedals so that even my butt doesn't get too sore, but it's real hard to get used to the *idea* of riding that great a distance.

And even greater than the physical benefits of being able to ride 100 miles in a day, is simply knowing that I can ride 100 miles. That knowledge alone has sustained me many times during the race season.

By mid-March my long road-training rides stretch into solo Saturday morning Century Rides along the Big Sur coast, or along the wine country of the Alexander Valley. At the end of the ride Marc would be waiting for me by the side of the road in our beat-up old VW bus, and during the slow chug of our drive back home he'd rub my legs, choose a quiet place for dinner, and listen while I recounted the details of every mile. Out there against the wind, deep into the drops of my bar, the question of what I hope to accomplish during the upcoming season arises. There are no distractions along the winding road, and I maintain my cadence until I arrive at some answers. During some of these Century Rides, I have resolved to become a better jumper. The season I won my first World Cup, I decided on a new race strategy from start to finish. Many times the answer doesn't concern racing at all. Rather, during some rides I have discovered that I wish Marc would ask me to marry him, or that I should go back to Baltimore and help my mother in her garden or listen to my dad talk about his plans to add a deck and screened porch to the beach house. There is always an answer during a Century Ride.

You don't have to be a pro cyclist to find the rewards from or answers during a Century Ride. One hundred years ago what the League of American Wheelmen, America's oldest cycling club, found during a Century Ride, recreational riders could find satisfying today.

The health and fitness benefits of being in good-enough shape to ride a Century are obvious, but still worth stating. The latest studies from the Institute of Medicine recommend that we all exercise vigorously for 1 hour a day. Unfortunately, government studies show that few of us actually follow that recommendation. "Obesity is a critical public health problem in our country that causes millions of Americans to suffer unnecessary health problems and to die prematurely," testified the Secretary of Health and Human Services at a Senate subcommittee hearing where he announced that Medicare officials are considering the designation of obesity itself as an illness. Realistically, one can see why. Huge segments of our adult population drive to work, work longer than they should at a job that doesn't provide much of a cardiovascular benefit, and then sit in traffic during the drive home again only to watch TV for an hour or two before sleep. That's the cycle for most of us. Obesity, heart disease, adult-onset diabetes, hypertension, and some cancers all are on the rise. Though the weekend could be an opportunity to stem those trends, too many of us still find ourselves "working" and not working out even if we do manage to squeeze in some gardening or throwing the ball around with the kids. Or, rather than exercising, we attempt to recover from the previous workweek by sleeping in and lounging, hoping to emerge on Monday morning, re-energized.

This desire to nest at home is very compelling. It's a comfort late at night as we stare at the mesmerizing infomercials for home gyms wrapped up in rubber bands that will eliminate fat from our thighs and hips as easily as they squeeze calories from our grocery list. Corporations, small-time inventors, and the federal government are all making huge investments in national chains of gyms and health spas with their pseudoherbal pharmaceuticals and weight loss centers. But we don't need all that.

We should be able to make the investment in ourselves to maintain our health and well-being, and riding a bike an hour or so a couple of days a week with the occasional longer ride during the weekend can have a huge payoff. Besides, Americans currently take fewer annual vacation days, less than 12, than any other industrial nation in the world. That's a trend that will be hard to turn around, but the average American could more easily take a stress-reducing hour's worth of vacation a couple of days a week by riding a bike along a rails-to-trails scenic byway, through a state park, or just home from work via a surface road.

If the recreational rider were able to get on a Century Ride training program, it would be a lot easier to actually ride up New Hampshire's Mount Washington, or around Nevada's Lake Tahoe when the opportunity for a weekend getaway presented itself. Maybe there would be a basic fitness level that would enable one to take full advantage of a lift pass and ski all day in Vail or Mount Snow. A hike in and out along the Grand Canyon's Bright Angel Trail wouldn't sound ridiculous. Riding a bike a few times a week is easy, and a Century Ride training program perhaps would make it even easier to maintain that healthy lifestyle a lot longer than will a video-based aerobic balance ball/step class/rubber band resistance regimen, or an all-grapefruit diet, or a TV ministry "pray your weigh to less!" program.

Even if someone is new to cycling and hopes to complete only one Century Ride as a personal accomplishment, realizing that goal is a great step toward other personal accomplishments like running a marathon or reaching a targeted weight loss goal. Perhaps you don't know what you want to do afterward, but don't forget, during that Century Ride there's a good chance the answers will come to you.

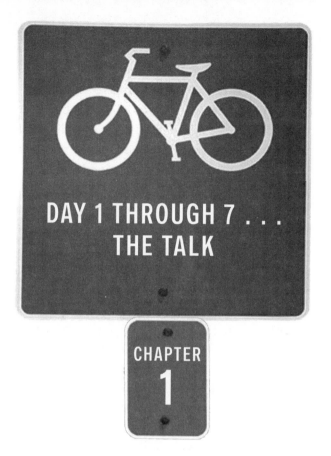

DAY 1 THROUGH 7 . . . THE TALK

CHAPTER 1

When I first told my good friend Rachel Lloyd, queen of the Day La Marin 100-mile mountain bike ride, that I was writing a book about how to train for a Century Ride, she laughed.

"You don't have to read a book to learn how to ride a Century," she giggled. "You just have to ride a lot."

Of course Rachel is right. But if it were that easy, everyone would do it. I merely hope this book helps.

How I Talked Dave into Trying a Century Ride

No reason at this point to tell my brother, Dave, I was thinking Century Ride. I was just asking, "Let's go for a ride, huh; you want to?" Standing astride the top tube of my bike, though the early spring sun still had little strength, I was warm enough, having already ridden nearly an hour from my home on a sailboat in Baltimore's Fells Point out of the city to the driveway in front of Dave's house near Loch Raven Reservoir. I imagined Dave in his office studio down in the basement hunched over his desktop. You would think that there would be only a binary response to a question like that . . . do you want to go for a bike ride?

Either, "Yes, I want to" or "No, don't want to." The cell phone connection chirped and warbled a bit. Either yes or no, a go or a no go, a one or a zero. Dave thinks in ones and zeros all day. So it would be just a simple binary response. While waiting for Dave to say something, my eyes wandered over the neat siding of his house, the ordered location of each window, and the proportional sizes of his shrubberies. Okay, one could imagine a response of ones and zeros, an endless string of Yes, No, Yes, No, No, No, Yes, No, Yes, Yes; a random sample of binary equivocations that could only be translated as "maybe later." The respondent doesn't want to say No. Not really. Who wouldn't rather chuck their workstation for a workout? But they don't imagine that they actually have the power to just say Yes, either. So the answer becomes a string of yeses and no's partly due to proclivity, protocol, and politeness and therefore open to misinterpretation. The Japanese have refined the art of clearly meaning No by politely saying, "That is not possible at this time." In real life, I've recently found out that among all levels of cycling ability this binary string can be infinitely longer than a century.

I kept the phone to my ear, hoping it wouldn't grow too warm while waiting for Dave's response.

Occasionally, when pressed to go for a ride by a few of my training partners, I've come up with some big "binarisms" myself. Even when the promise is a fun ride or just a peek at the course of some upcoming race, my excuses can start flying.

And yet a widely accepted training dictum is that to become a stronger rider, you should not only ride, but ride with stronger riders. Riding with someone stronger isn't easy; that's where the doubt comes in.

Mark Weir is one of the strongest pro riders the hills of Marin

County have ever produced. You would know that just by looking at him. First impression is that he's either the world's most buff roadie or its skinniest carcass-chucking free rider. Certainly there are faster riders around, but nobody else has promised an all-the-bells-and-whistles Santa Cruz Blur to anybody who can even finish one of his 10,000-feet-of-climbing Death Rides. This more-than-healthy-appearing Bruce Willis look-alike holds the record for the Downieville Downhill MTB race, numerous singlespeed XC titles, and other legendary Saturday morning road ride triumphs up Mount Tamalpais. I really wanted to ride a lot with Weir, but I could handle only about one ride a week with him. More than one big ride a week wouldn't leave me enough time between rides to properly recover. I didn't want it to appear obvious that I was just hanging on. Sure, a little bit of vanity perhaps, but looking strong on a training ride is also an issue of sanity.

A critical component of a long training ride is the mental aspect. At the finish of a training ride with Weir, I wanted to think that I had kicked some ass. That I had taken my share of pulls, led some climbs, and been able to respond when he friskily attacked. After a ride with him, I certainly didn't want to be crawling up to the massage table, whimpering, and recoiling the next morning when the phone rang, terrified that it was Weir inviting me to take another beating. Also I didn't want to lose a smidgen of any thinly sliced psychological edge that I might have had over my competitors. The thought that one of my competitors would be able to recall the confidence from a mechanic whose buddy had overheard the chuckle from another rider's soigneur, the slander of a club rider who had been in a coffee shop and had heard the whisper from a smarmy Cat 1 barista that Mark Weir had dropped me that morning like a slippery bar of soap on every climb was as dangerous to my racing psyche as though I were balanced on the starting line in mismatched socks. A painted bird like that would be torn apart by the peloton, I imagined. So, in order to beg out of some rides with Weir I have strung out a tangle of yes/no responses myself.

And I am guilty of a few other excuses, too. Once, I changed cell phone plans and regrettably lost the number of that guy who wanted to talk to me about the Ride Across America. Oops. It can go the other way, too. When I annually offer to put in some training miles with Alison Dunlap to help her prepare for the Redlands Classic, she usually thanks me but apologizes, "That is not possible at this time."

Consequently, when talking to my brother Dave about getting together for a long ride, I thought I was prepared to tease an ultimate yes from his binary loops. But I was caught off guard by Dave's reality: that of a father with two kids, the supportive husband of a busy wife with her own demanding business, and the responsibilities his own computer company created. And not enough hours in the day.

Marin County, where I have enjoyed the most of my riding and where I invented and contended with the majority of excuses not to ride, is a special place. I've homesteaded on the fringes of it in a leaky sailboat and then in a little cottage on a dirt road in the woods, but in the beautifully landscaped heart of Marin most homeowners are free from economic concerns and free to ride. Responsible house sitters, a demographic that I admittedly have more in common with, are in big demand and are courted as though they were celebrities. The residents of Marin ride their bikes a lot, but they do work, in their own fashion. The renters and house sitters work at occasional jobs: bartending, Kinkoing, mortgage brokering, etc. And if they really want to go for a ride, they just don't show up for work.

A lot of Marin's homeowners, it seems, work on "projects." I never really figured out how one got involved in a "project" that would allow you to ride a bike a lot *and* buy a 3 bed, 3.5 ba, granite counters, stainless appliances, off st. pkg, sunny hillside, 2 bridge bay views, craftsman w/wraparound decks and hot tub in Sausalito. But, I've ridden with some people whose projects were things like consulting at the Gene Bank Savings and Clone or the menu development for a nationwide chain of natural food markets. On projects like these it is perfectly acceptable to tell your project director that you're taking a sabbatical to climb K2 or help a buddy edit an indie film.

I didn't know the proper way to respond to Dave's excuses when I called him out of whimsy on sunny mornings to see if he wanted to ride for a couple hours before lunch. I didn't know how to parry his responses like, "Marla, I'd love to go for a bike ride, but this customer just bounced a huge check on me. He's not answering his phone and his Web site is down."

I'd counter Dave with something that usually worked in Marin like, "Oh, okay. How about after lunch?" One of our cell phones would then inexplicably drop its connection.

After living for a few weeks in Baltimore, it was dawning on me that there were people who simply didn't have the time to go on a bike ride. It was outrageous.

Okay, I am now riding in the real world. I'll have to adapt.

So, when Dave would say that he couldn't ride with me again, I'd venture out alone and attempt to salvage the afternoon with what I call mountain bike urban assaults. This would boil down to bunny-hopping onto the rusty steel bollards along the Inner Harbor's water-front. Maybe showing off a little for some disinterested tourists with my only street trick—a handlebar spin that is only intriguing to wit-nesses because it's doubtful each time that I can pull it off. I'd finish off the sunlight by riding the lippy dirt jumps found in abandoned lots between the formstone row houses whose brick facades were yet to be repointed in the next wave of speculative rehabbing, although I'm not too crazy about the flat tires caused by dirty syringes.

Anyway, Dave and I finally did finagle a sunny spring afternoon while his boys were off at a chess club thing and Lorena, his thank-fully understanding wife, was swamped with her preparations for an upcoming trade show.

Dave's in pretty good physical shape for a 40-something guy car-rying a mortgage and two college saving plans for his kids. In the spandex of a cycling jersey, the spare tube he carries in the back pocket definitely bulges out more than the one he carries in the front. Public opinion is not yet clamoring that he pull on baggy shorts in-stead of chamois. Still, on our first ride he led out from his garage up the hill of his driveway and out into the street. Too hard and too fast.

I almost couldn't stay on his wheel for that first hot minute, but as the miles rolled under, so did he. We fought a couple good stop sign sprints. He knew the route, though, and planned his attacks with cunning. Dave's a gamer. I'd almost forgotten how much of one. In no time at all we were time-traveling back to when he had pimples and I was bereft of breasts. Trackstanding for traffic at intersections, we jabbed each other with elbows while still exchanging pleasantries in a conversational tone. Even though our breaths were deep, the laughing was deeper.

We're separated in age by about 6 years, but the distance can seem greater than that. I moved away out West years ago, whereas his home is 15 minutes from our childhood tree house. He's very happily married with wonderful kids while I'm too chicken to allow my boyfriend of 10 years now, Marc, the opportunity to even pop the big question. Lately, I've been Green Party liberal, and Dave, well, Dave's not. I'm Mac; he's Windows. Dave has an appreciation for large parcel subdivisions in high-scoring school districts, with strong homeowners' associations, stringent covenants, and deed restrictions that govern the color and material of front doors and window trim. Meanwhile, I find the gaudy, wild colors of the mismatched Victorians, Spanish Revival, and concrete contemporaries of San Francisco's cramped hills more appealing. I often prefer fat tires, and Dave is the proud owner of a sleek carbon fiber skinny tire bike once raced by Floyd Landis, the workhorse of the 2004 Tour de France's US Postal Team.

But, we both like to ride. And while riding with Dave, I really wanted to bridge some of the distances between us. But it was obvious that we weren't gonna cross any bridges together unless we agreed on some sort of program. Dave really enjoyed his time on the bike, but realistically it was hard to find the time. We needed some kind of structure that we could count on that allowed us the opportunity to ride together and both benefit. We needed a plan.

So, after our ride, while hogging back plastic jugs of blue Gatorade and snacking on salty treats on his deck, I casually suggested we come up with a riding plan. Dave didn't hear me the first time because his yellow lab, Jed, chose that moment to lick the cool, condensing water droplets that dripped down the neck of Dave's Gatorade bottle. I waited until Dave had wiped up the spilled electrolyte the way all brothers probably clean up spills: by trying to sop up the puddle stain with the not-very-absorbent rubber and stainless steel of his bike shoe. When he was satisfied that he had cleaned up the spill, I again casually mentioned that we should come up with a riding plan.

"Dave, you should ride a Century."

We each swallowed a mouthful of blue, flavored sodium water during the ensuing pause.

We were all alone at the house. In a flash, we were transported back to one of our tree houses, and Dave and I began to gush in conspiratorial whispers about which days he might be able to sneak in a ride. Which clients he could juggle at work. Mornings or afternoons? We both glanced over to Jed. Could he be trusted?

I love plans. Especially secret ones.

Dave fetched two beers from the kitchen ... and his fancy Treo, too.

Entering "Bike Ride" into his electronic secretary, and seeing the greenish glow of those letters conferred legitimacy on Tues, Thurs, and Sat from 1:00 P.M. to 3:00 P.M. I climbed up onto the arm of his Adirondack chair so I could see the handheld's screen over his shoulder. We both admired his data entry. Bike Ride was now a subject heading as much a weighty part of his weekly routine as Kids' Scouting and Wed Eve's Entrepreneur Club.

Dave looks a little bit like Jerry Seinfeld without the curly hair. Dave's hair is as dark, but shorter with maybe just a few more gray strands 'cause Jerry probably dyes his. But more than looking like him, Dave has an impish quality as though he's suppressing a subversive thought that Seinfeld is paid millions to express.

"Hey Dave, type in Century Ride," I urged in the perky tones of my best imitation of Elaine's toothy smile. "Go ahead." Seinfeld's Elaine does have much better hair though, I admit. "There's a Century Ride in the Blue Ridge Mountains not far from here this June."

Dave's eyebrows were now arched to the brim of his brow trying to contain all the subversive elements of this riding plan. He had plenty of opportunity to string out some rationalizations. Instead, he typed in the letters and then we started to conspire until the sun lost its strength, and we didn't stop until we heard the crunch of Lorena's radials rolling down the driveway. We both cradled the bottles and pretzel crumbs and slipped through the glass slider into the kitchen to dispose of any incriminating evidence. Just as the side door opened and the hardwood floors squeaked with the footfalls of the kids' tennis shoes, Dave tossed his organizer into a corner of the Corian and I casually slid onto a counter stool. We both affected an air of nonchalance as Lorena breezed into the kitchen, smiling, "Marla! What a nice surprise!"

I hadn't finished my beer, so I was pretty clearheaded during my ride from Dave's back into the city. I knew some things then about our plan to train for and ride a Century this summer that Dave couldn't possibly know. I knew that we were two very different riders, myself a professional and Dave not even a club rider. That we each would train along two very different plans. I knew that we'd be able to ride together only as much as those two plans intersected. That'd be once or twice a week at the most. Still, I was happy that riding together as little as that would have great rewards for the both of us.

The training plan for him, the one that we thumbnail-sketched that afternoon, would be developed in much more detail with spreadsheets, multicolored cells, and calendar entries on his desktop. That plan would in all likelihood be tough to stick to. Such is the nature of most plans. I had learned that myself, and I knew that Dave would come to find out.

Dave's Training Log— Week 1

Date	Sleep/Wt.	Workout	Notes
Mon	6 hrs/165		
Tues	8 hrs/167		
Wed	7.5 hrs/168	1.5 hrs; 27 miles; easy to mod. pace	Legs stale from sitting all day
Thu	9 hrs/169		
Fri	5 hrs/168		(Scouts: chasing kids all night!)
Sat	10 hrs/168	30 min	Not much time—easy ride
Sun	9 hrs/169	1 hr: easy to mod. pace	

Total Riding Hours: **3**
Total Miles: **60**

Marla's Training Log— Week 1

Date	Sleep/Wt.	Workout	Notes
Mon	7 hrs/140	3 hrs: zone 2*	Felt tired from traveling, legs heavy, so spun in low gear
Tue	9.5 hrs/139	1.5 hrs: zone 2	Good energy, pretty flat roads
Wed	8 hrs/139	2 hrs: zones 2–4 mtb ride; 8x5 min intervals at threshold (ff170 BPM)	Had endless power and energy; excellent conditions, went sailing in afternoon—too many margaritas
Thu	9 hrs/140	1 hr: zone 1	Tired and sluggish, arms and legs sore from yesterday
Fri	6 hrs/140	2 hrs: zones 2–4 3x5 min intervals; efforts in upper zone 4	Felt decent, but sloppy form
Sat	12 hrs/138	2.5 hrs: zones 3 & 5 Hilly mtb ride with 20x sprints	Worked on technique
Sun	9 hrs/139	30 min hike: zone 1	Noticed flu bug

Total Hours: **12.5**

* For an explanation of the training zones, see poage 38.

DAY 8 THROUGH 14 . . .
THE IDEAL TRAINING
PLAN

CHAPTER
2

Whether you're like Dave, a real-job working stiff with just a bike in the garage, or like me, in between "projects" and lucky enough to have a whole quiver of bikes, you can still benefit from our ideal training plan. So, the first thing you do to prepare for a Century Ride is get onto your computer and open up your spreadsheet program. If you don't have the slick software, you can simply copy the column heads on page 20 onto another piece of paper. Then tape it to the fridge where you'll see it and fill it out every day.

Sample Training Log

A training log is an important way to track your progress. It also will help motivate you to stick to your program, as any blank spaces will drive you crazy. When you look back, you'll find patterns that can

Devising the training plan

help you adjust your training or figure out why you might have gotten sick. Some people also have columns for other variables like weather, bike maintenance, and excuses. The more data, the better.

Date

Sleep/Weight

Workout: Type, location, time, intensity

Notes: overall feeling, food intake

The first week or two of the ideal 100-Day Training Plan for a Century Ride is similar for Dave and me. Of course, consideration has been made for our relative strengths as cyclists. Starting out the year, even world-class racers like Lance Armstrong begin a training cycle quite like the plan outlined below, perhaps varying only in distance. Distance is easily quantifiable. Depending on your level of fitness and cycling ability, your training plan can certainly be more ambitious, but it need not be. The important thing is to draw up a plan similar to the one below so that you can deviate from it. It's also okay if you stick to it exactly as outlined if you want. But it is important to note the distinction between deviating from the plan and obviating the plan. You obviate the plan if you're not riding at all by week 2.

By week 2 you just have to ride your bike. That's called implementing the plan. Just get on your bike and ride. This plan takes into account a number of contingencies, for example, not riding on Day 5 because you've spent way too much time fiddling around with either your spreadsheet or your adhesive tape, depending on your ability with either. You also have plenty of time prior to week 2 to thumb through bike magazines checking out cool stuff. Factored into this timeline is the opportunity to spend money at your local bike shop on toys you think you'll need. There is at least one afternoon allocated to bragging to friends and co-workers that you are already in fact on a training program! Accommodation has been set aside for one day of not feeling well in addition to one 24-hour period of inclement weather. Provisions have been made for mechanical as well as psychological setbacks. As you can see, the training plan up to week 2 is very comprehensive. But then by week 2 you just have to ride.

Even the most serious athlete at the beginning of the season should ease into the workouts. For me, it's always been best that my first training sessions are light. The rationale for dipping a toe instead of belly flopping into these every-other-day rides is twofold.

I ride my bike nearly every day, even during the extreme off season like the winter holidays, but that doesn't mean I can just throw myself into a workout. I'm usually dragging a B.O.B. trailer full of groceries around the neighborhood or pulling my wheezy boyfriend to the local movie theater. Those miles in the off season are junk miles, which never add to the quality of my fitness. One saving grace of those miles is the "air that is spared." I don't count these miles as training miles.

During that first week that precedes the actual riding part, I begin my training by eating the foods that my body will need to sustain my training efforts. I wean myself from the junk food that my body has become used to. I don't make the change cold turkey, though. My diet on the whole is healthy, except for nightly sweets. I'm too cheap to all at once throw out a half gallon of ice cream, packages of cookies, and sleeves of red licorice twists. Nope. I savor every bit for that week, eat it all up until it's gone, replacing those nasty treats in turn with sorbet, Luna bars, and fresh or dried fruits, so that by the morning of my first riding day, my body is purged, prepped, and poised for peak performance. It's what my body wants, so it's easy to do.

Marc is the cook in the house, and he's big on grilling free-range chicken and wild fresh fish and lean cuts of grass-fed beef. Marc makes an effort to incorporate lots of fruits and nuts into his meals. The vegetables seem to take care of themselves. Marc doesn't like to cook with canned goods or frozen bags. He insists on real butter, but sparingly. We use the whipped kind, so that each gob balanced on the flat edge of a butter knife seems as large as a small scoop of ice cream because of the extra volume of air. And we only use sea salt as a garnish to rim one-half of the occasional margarita glass. We do eat out. Never any fast food, though. I just keep an eye on the portion sizes, making sure that they're relative to my daily calorie burn. When I start training, I find that my portion sizes increase. Or I may snack on Clif Bars or protein shakes; my body wants me to know that I need the extra food.

If it has been your custom to fall asleep after the late night talk shows on TV while still managing to drag yourself out of bed early in the morning to start your day, the addition of a vigorous bike ride a couple of times a week can easily push you into the realm of walking zombie. You might think that's a sacrifice you're willing to make, but please don't subject others around you to that. What you have to sacrifice is the late-night TV, or the midnight Internet, or the vampire club scene. My own trouble is that I usually get a burst of creative energy just as the sun sets, and that's when I want to repaint the bathroom walls, or download milk crates of music into my iPod, or total up my monthly travel expenses. Like with your eating habits, make a gradual transition. During the first week, I try to crawl under the covers a half hour earlier each night.

Eight to 10 hours a night is the minimum amount of sleep if you want to be physically active. You might argue that there is no way you can lie in bed that long. The demands of your life are so great that you're pressed for time just winking by on 6 hours a night right now. Just try going to sleep a little earlier each night. Don't worry so much about your hectic schedule, and you might find that after a week or two, because you're now enjoying the proper amount of sleep, you find more energy and drive during the day, making you more productive. Laboring on at work and struggling through at home by depriving yourself of needed sleep is the equivalent of junk miles on the bike: There is no net gain.

Since my fitness level is higher than Dave's, the warmup ride out to his house worked out really well. Dave wanted to ride, but his youngest boy, Jeremy, accidentally ate some dairy and his face swelled up. I arrived at his door ready to ride, but Dave had to tell me that "it was not possible at this time."

A couple days later, Jeremy felt better and Dave felt better about riding because of that. The ride started out with an air of gritty determination about it, since this was the first day of training. I tried to pierce this purposefulness by riding as often as possible with no hands on my bar.

Dave caught on and lightened up. He usually rides alone. Which is fine, except that he misses out on one of the best features of riding your bike. Though at times cycling can be an inherently solitary pursuit, like the time trial, invariably more rewarding is the social aspect of riding with a buddy, in a group. Or even with your little sister.

We rode at a steadier tempo than during our previous rides. I cautioned Dave to make an effort to rein in his jackrabbit starts. Enjoy the benefits of a warmup, which can be anywhere from 15 to 30 minutes, depending on your fitness.

Everyone should stretch a little before even hopping on the bike. But so few of us do. I'm often guilty of this sin of omission. I couldn't imagine that Dave had the peace and quiet in his busy house to sit on the floor and stretch. So getting him to warm up properly would be something we'd have to work on.

Your first few rides should not be a pain fest. Do not make that easy mistake.

Surprisingly, it takes quite a bit of self-discipline to not overdo it on the first day. Out on the road on that first day, squinting through fresh Oakleys or your just-out-of-the-plastic-bag jersey, cleaner now than it will ever be again, the adrenaline will begin to drip and the endorphins will start to dope you into imagining that you are a cycling machine.

Tomorrow morning you'll be sore. That's why the following day is essentially an off day. Overdoing it can happen to all athletes. If you read the sports page, it's no coincidence that more injuries occur during the preseason of football and baseball relative to the actual season. We all know weekend warriors who can go all out for the first month or two of the softball or surfing summer, but usually those warriors are unable to sustain that frenetic level of activity during the whole year. The little nagging sprains and scrapes soon sideline, them and it should be no surprise.

In the training plan, every other day as an "off" day means different things for different riders. For Dave it meant, off—off the bike. Do not pass go; do not ride. Off.

Personally, for the purposes of this book, the second day for me means quite another thing. And it involves a little trick.

I planned and schemed and scratched my head conjuring up some way that Dave and I could share the same plan to train together for a Century Ride. What I wanted to avoid was the parallax of ski trips Marc and I have shared. Packing for those ski weekends, I always imagined that I would have the patience and composure to snowplow down the bunny trail with Marc. The bunny trail actually worries me, because I find myself imagining the toddlers in snowsuits to be fixed objects that I can jump, or slalom through, or ricochet past. The bunny trail is at the upper end of Marc's skiing ability, though he does have a special talent for crouching in a low aero tuck and can reach an incredibly high rate of speed over a short distance until his ski tips encounter a mogul or a tree. After a few "hot runs" like that, Marc usually props his sprained knee on a picnic bench or hoists a draft beer with a wrenched elbow and spends the rest of his Day Pass at the Lodge looking through binoculars for my dangerous Picabo Street swooshes down the double-black-diamond runs. It's never the same ski weekend for the both of us.

For Dave it would be a plan that consisted of 1 day on and 1 day off. For me too, except that during my true off days I'd ride with Dave. The days he had off and wasn't riding at all would be my on days. That way, I could train hard by myself or with stronger riding partners and not worry about Dave struggling to keep up. He would be recovering for the next day's effort, and he'd be ready to ride with me

Dave's Ideal Training Plan—Week 2

Dave's Goal: Introduce training routine and low-intensity base miles

Date	Workout	Intensity	Notes
Mon	Off		
Tue	1.0 hr ride	Easy, zones 1–2	
Wed	Home gym—30 min		Situps, pushups, squats
Thu	1.5 hr ride	Easy, zone 2	
Fri	Off		
Sat	Off		Activity with kids
Sun	2.0 hr ride		In zone 3 with Marla
Total proposed workout hours: **5**			

Marla's Ideal Training Plan—Week 2

Marla's Goal: Continue typical training routine adding base miles; work with Dave on his new program

Date	Workout	Intensity	Notes
Mon	1 hr	Easy spin	Recovery, zones 1–2
Tue	2 hr ride	Moderate hills, zones 2–3	
Wed	Gym 1 hr, spin 1 hr legs, abs, back		
Thu	2 hr ride	Easy, zone 2	
Fri	30 min spin	Recovery	
Sat	2.0 hr ride		
Sun	2.5 hr group ride	Higher intensity— zones 2–3 moderate, zones 2–3 w/a few hills with Dave	

Total proposed workout hours: **12**

during my off day, when I would be able to ride at his pace with no detriment to my professional training goals.

The on-off inversion would really benefit us both. Dave would gain by riding with someone stronger. Just as I had to work harder to keep up with Mark Weir. And I would be better off riding with Dave during my slower recovery days. Too often, some flashy roadie flicks past me when I'm alone and I can't help it, so I sink into my bar, click into a bigger gear, and grind him down until he's dust on the road behind me . . . or I blow up trying, anyway.

This every-other-day plan will also save you from mentally burning out. It prevents you from developing any contempt for your road bike that you might already be feeling for your computer screen at work. It's truly amazing what the human body can do if the brain gets out of the way. Dave will never ride a Century if, after a couple of rides, he dreads pulling his bike off the rack. He'll never be able to ride for 5 hours or more if he begins to resent the miles ahead. Taking those every other days off will allow Dave to recover a bit, to break the riding routine and play with the kids instead.

The pitfall of some training plans is that once you're off track, you're lost forever. It's the Tyranny of the Timetable. The Bossiness of the Bar Graph. The Lack of Penitence of the Pie Chart. Like in school when you're studying French, each day of each week is predicated on having learned the prior lessons. Lesson plans usually all lack one important element found in this book. That is the Stop Time Feature.

I didn't want Dave becoming discouraged about missing a couple of training rides and then shrugging his shoulders about his plan. I didn't want my brother to feel like I had at times, like I was in *I Love Lucy* working on the candy conveyor belt as it inexorably ramped up, leaving me behind with a mouthful of chocolate. No. If Dave missed a ride, he wouldn't be lost. All he had to do to get back on track was use the Stop Time Feature. He could freeze the plan and ride the next day on his off day. Then the plan would resume as though Dave had never hit a bump in the road at all.

Dave's Actual Training Log — Week 2

Date	Sleep/Wt.	Workout	Notes
Mon	6 hrs/165		
Tue	9 hrs/167	1 hr: easy	Relaxing ride
Wed	7 hrs/168		Couldn't work out in gym— computer meltdown
Thu	7 hrs/169	1.5 hrs: moderate	Good ride
Fri	5 hrs/168		
Sat	10 hrs/168		
Sun	9 hrs/169	2.0 hrs	Felt great

Total Riding Hours: **4.5**
Total Miles: **73**

Marla's Actual Training Log—Week 2

Date	Sleep/Wt.	Workout	Notes
Mon	8 hrs/140	1 hr: zone 2	Felt sick, fluish; turned around early and went home
Tue	9.5 hrs/139	1.5 hrs: zones 1–2 Gym: 30 min upper body and back	Decent energy Rode to gym; good strength
Wed	10 hrs/139	5 hrs: zones 1–2 1 hr trailwork	Felt better Strenuous digging/ hiking
Thu	9 hrs/140	5 hrs: zones 2–4 2.5 hrs mtb, working on power (3x5 min efforts), 2.5 hrs p.m. road ride, with 1.5 hrs at easier pace with Dave—legs loaded	
Fri	9 hrs/141	1.5 hrs: zone 2	Easy road ride, running errands. Got ticket from running a stop sign— should have run away.
Sat	7 hrs/141	2 hrs: zone 3 & 5	Felt fresh, 20x sprints. Worked on snap. Good warmup/cooldown.
Sun	7 hrs/ 139	1.5 hrs: zone 1	Felt horrible, not enough sleep

Total Hours: **17.5**

DAY 15 THROUGH 21 . . . . HOW TO SET UP A TRAINING PLAN

CHAPTER

3

Dave and I hadn't built anything together since he started to become interested in girls. That was the same summer that I started to wear a training bra, so obviously, everything was changing for me that summer. One of the hardest adjustments I had to deal with was that my older brothers would no longer have anything to do with me. Oh, they were still nice to me. They still talked to me when they had to. But I was just no longer as close to them as I had been during the spring. That they would no longer let me build anything with them was the cruelest blow. They ceased including me in the conspiracy of dragging all that booty down by the river along whose low banks we had always built forts. I had loved building those forts in the woods. A new, ramshackle tree fort each summer.

So it's been years since Dave and I started building a new project. That's why now, constructing a Century Ride training plan for Dave was so much fun for me. During a week of e-mails, a couple of short afternoon rides, and one backyard barbecue, we worked out the basic 100-Day Training Plan for a Century Ride for Dave. And a plan for me, too. His plan was supposed to enable him to finish a Century Ride. My plan was to share some bike rides with him and enhance my level of fitness.

Dave's goal was reasonable and attainable: finishing his first Century Ride. Under 7 hours would be a total and absolute victory for him. My goal was not only to ride with him as much as I could during his 100 days of training, but with luck, to sink the "love of cycling" hook deep under his skin. That way we would be riding together for many days, and hopefully years, afterward.

Racing bikes for 10 years professionally has humbled me in many respects. One crumb that I have swallowed repeatedly over the years is that there is no such thing as the perfect training plan. If there was a perfect plan, everybody would follow it, and we'd all be winners.

In a Century Ride every cyclist is different. Each person is beginning the ride from a unique place. For a few, the goal is to win. For many, the desire is a crack at the top 10, perhaps a personal best. Still, most are proud just to have finished. And many are simply happy to discover how hard they could try.

The cycling goals that we may have are not universally shared. Some may want to win a local criterium or a stage race. Maybe the goal is just to move up from Cat 2 to Cat 1 or to make the varsity squad of your college cycling team. Maybe what you really want is to ride well enough to score some *swag* from your local bike shop. Maybe all you want to do is be able to hang with a buddy when he goes for his weekly rides. After recognizing that you want to achieve any of these goals, you need to come up with a plan. The goals of any particular cyclist may be individual, but the components of a training plan are nearly universal. In that sense, Dave's 100-Day Training Plan for a Century Ride is not that different from a training plan to simply ride faster than that guy in your Saturday group ride with the Lance Armstrong signature Trek who drives you crazy every time he talks

DAVE'S 100-DAY TRAINING PLAN

Week	Phase	Mon	Tues	Wed
1	Intro	Off	30 min/easy	Off
2	Buildup	Off	1 hr/easy	30 min/easy
3	Mod intensity	Off	30 min/easy	Off
4	Recovery	Off	1 hr/easy	Off
5	Base	1 hr/easy	Off	1 hr/easy
6	Buildup	1 hr/easy	Off	1.5 hr/mod
7	Intensity	Off	1 hr/mod	Off
8	Recovery	Off	45 min/easy	Off
9	Base	1 hr/easy	Off	1.5 hr/mod
10	Buildup	1 hr/easy	Off	1.75 hr/mod
11	Intensity	Off	1 hr/easy	Off
12	Recovery	Off	1 hr/easy	Off
13	Preride	1 hr/easy	Off	1 hr/mod
14	Taper	Off	1 hr/easy	Off
15	CENTURY	1hr/easy	Off	1 hr/hard
16	Recovery	Off	1 hr/easy	Off

about bagging the big cols during his 2-week trip to France last summer.

There are some principles that all successful training plans adhere to. Although a training plan takes you from where you are to the realization of your goal, formulating your plan works backward instead. Developing a training plan starts with the goal and recounts the steps from there, back to where you're starting from.

Dave owns a bike. A really nice bike. He bought it off an e-Bay seller. It's a former US Postal Team training bike that Floyd Landis used to ride. The geometry even fits Dave pretty well. But he doesn't ride it much. Just not enough time. And besides, he considers the bike

FOR A CENTURY RIDE

Thu	Fri	Sat	Sun
30 min/easy	Off	Off	1 hr/mod
1.5 hrs/easy	Off	Off	2 hrs/mod
45 min/mod	Off	Off	2 hrs/mod
1 hr/easy	Off	1.5 hrs/easy	Off
Off	1.5 hr/mod	Off	Off
Off	Off	Off	2 hrs/mod
1.5 hrs/easy	Off	Off	2 hrs/hard
1 hr/easy	Off	1.5 hrs/mod	Off
Off	Off	1.5 hrs/mod	Off
Off	1 hr/easy	Off	2.5 hrs/mod
1.5 hr/mod	Off	Off	2 hrs/hard
1.5 hrs/easy	Off	2 hrs/mod	Off
Off	30 min/easy	Off	5 hrs/mod
1.5 hrs/mod	Off	1.5 hrs/hard	Off
Off	1 hr/easy	Off	CENTURY
1.5 hrs/easy	Off	Off	1.5 hrs/easy

as much an art piece, or an heirloom, as he does a piece of exercise equipment.

Dave had already figured out his goal: finishing a Century. The next step, determining his baseline fitness, took us only two quick afternoon rides.

First, we figured out how heavily he was breathing at a moderate pace. And the second indicator was determining how much he was whining toward the end of his rides. Very scientific.

Dave is an active guy, but even he couldn't say he was ripped. That's not something Lorena would say, anyway. When we were kids, Dave was always skinny. Lean is maybe a better word. And now in his mid-forties, he has thickened up just a tiny bit. We just guessed at how much he had fallen from his college physique by adding up his increases in his waist size: an inch increase in size for every 10 years since he graduated.

For our purposes, we quantified baseline fitness as a measure of how many miles he could ride in a 15-minute period. Fitness can be measured any number of ways. It could be estimated by his average speed and endurance. That's relatively easy to determine. We could measure his power output and max VO_2 tested at a lab somewhere, but then it gets complicated.

I should really have let Dave borrow my heart rate (HR) monitor to estimate his fitness, but because he once broke my Barbie sing-a-melody radio when I was little, I refrained. I train with a monitor during some parts of the season, and during other parts I go without. It's a useful tool. The HR monitor really lets you accurately monitor your intensity zones. Instead, I just asked him to check his waking heart rate the next morning with his built-in heart rate monitor: his index finger.

I told him the lower his waking heart rate is, the more efficient his heart is. That's a good indicator of fitness. Then we looked at a chart and figured out how to calculate his maximum heart rate. With that number, we could figure out what his intensity zones would be. A heart rate monitor is not absolutely necessary in order to utilize intensity zone training, but it does eliminate some of the guesswork. Simply relying on mileage ridden or hours in the saddle is insufficient as a means to track your training.

It is commonly understood that athletic gains are not made all at once. Rather, over time from a baseline of fitness, a progressive loading of training intensity is introduced. The intensity zones, either with or without the use of a heart rate monitor, can be a fairly accurate method for assuring progressiveness of these training loads. The intensity zones allow cyclists to safely follow their programs, while steadily approaching their goals. A common training blunder is riding for sustained periods at the same intensity, where the highs aren't high enough, and the lows aren't low enough. You must pay careful attention to a proper recovery after any intense effort. Big gains are realized when you train at your "sweet spot," or anaerobic threshold. This is about 80 to 90 percent of your maximum heart rate.

CALCULATING YOUR MAXIMUM HEART RATE

The Hard Way: To find your maximum heart rate the most accurate way, warm up for 15 to 20 minutes with a heart rate monitor on a day that you're feeling good. Find a challenging hill and think about the worst rush hour moment you've ever had. Hammer up the hill out of the saddle for 30 to 60 seconds, going as hard as possible until you practically collapse. Don't worry about form. Watch your monitor and remember the highest heart rate. That's your max!

The Easy Way: Calculate your maximum heart rate using the formula below. This doesn't require an HR monitor but isn't nearly as accurate as doing it the hard way.

Male:	**Female:**
220−Age (nonathletic)	226−Age (nonathletic)
205−Age/2 (already fit)	211−Age/2 (already fit)

Example: A fit 46-year-old male would find his max HR to be 182 beats per minute (BPM).

By using intensity zones, you can measure this cycle of progressively loading the intensity of your training sessions followed by a proper recovery. In Dave's case, his goal is riding a Century, and his season to train for it is 100 days long.

Through the use of periodized training in his plan, Dave would be able to achieve this goal. *Periodization* is a big word. But it's not a big deal. Periodization is simply breaking up your training program into four phases leading up to your big event. The phases are general conditioning, buildup, tapering to your peak, and recovery. Each one of these periods can further be divided into smaller, more specific periodized training blocks.

Here are some easy steps to follow to help you plan your periodized program.

Develop Your Ideal Training Plan

Step 1. Evaluate your fitness/last year's season.

- Have you been riding or exercising frequently?

- Do you maintain healthy eating habits? Be honest!

- Rate your strengths and weaknesses. How is your aerobic and anaerobic power? How is your flexibility? How do other people rate you?

- Get your body fat measured.

- Were your goals last year accomplished? Were they too far-reaching or too conservative?

- Did anything go wrong last year? Why?

Step 2. Set your goals.

- Be specific and realistic.

- Try to set long-term (2- to 3-year), seasonal (1-year), and intermediate (1- to 2-month) goals.

- Include several variables, like target body weight, race results, or simply finishing a Century.

Step 3. Design your training plan.

- Use either a calendar, graph paper, a notebook, or a computer spreadsheet.

- Fill in the big race/ride dates and work backward from the date you would like to peak.

- Divide the season into four training cycles (three buildup to one recovery), and each of these into four periods with the same ratio.

- Start out from your baseline with a General Conditioning Phase.

- Then add a Progressive Buildup Phase.

- Follow it by a Taper.

- That leads to a Peak Performance Phase.

- End with a Recovery Phase.

- Make sure your plan is progressive, keeping in mind the big picture.

Dave in his element, working on the training plan

• Remember to include variation of load within the phases.

• A longer buildup will result in durability of form.

Step 4. Use your training log.

• A training log is a notebook, flow chart, or calendar in which you record the daily benchmarks of your training.

TRAINING ZONES WITH A HEART RATE MONITOR

Training in these zones is the recommended technique for gauging your efforts.

Zone	% of Max HR	Training
1	50–60	Low-Intensity Zone: Ridiculously easy, comfortable pace Good for recovery riding and running errands Can be done anytime
2	60–70	The Temperate Zone: Conversational pace with easy spinning Good for building solid base and endurance One or two days a week on long rides
3	70–80	The Aerobic Zone: More intense but not exhausting pace Good for working on tempo and building fitness Two or three rides a week, after building decent base

- The training log will allow you to discover patterns or trends in your training.

- It helps you stay on track with your training plan.

To start your periodized training plan, pencil in your cycling goal and its date on the calendar. Your training plan might be 100 days long

Zone	% of Max HR	Training
4	80–90	The Anaerobic Threshold Zone: Riding so hard that it's tough to breathe; legs burn Good for hill and hard work recovery; strengthening One or two shorter rides a week, after good base
5	90–100	Maximal Zone: Short sprinting at the redline; seeing stars Improves athletic performance One workout a week, after extensive training

like Dave's. If you're like most elite athletes, your plan will probably be 12 months long. This yearly plan is broken down into four periods, or seasons. The seasons are about 3 months long. These four seasons themselves are broken down into four blocks of 3 weeks each. The length of these periods and blocks may be customized, depending on your schedule and goals.

It's in this way a rider gets progressively better from year to year. This is how you see riders progress from promising juniors into the

TRAINING ZONES WITHOUT A HEART RATE MONITOR

This method is an alternative to using a HR monitor, although it's not as accurate.

Zone	Training	Rate of Perceived Exertion (RPE)
1	Light Intensity	Cruising, easy pace Breathing slightly labored, still conversational Approximately 60–70% max heart rate Recovery or endurance training
2	Moderate Intensity	Light to somewhat hard pace Breathing labored, talking in small snatches Approximately 70–85% max heart rate Good for hill training and strength
3	High Intensity	Hard to all-out effort Tough to maintain for long periods Approximately 85–100% max heart rate Great for intense workouts, high-end fitness

Based on the Rating of Perceived Exertion Scale (RPE), proposed by G.A. Borg

senior peloton. Training like this allows some riders in their late forties and beyond to enjoy great results at the expense of younger and stronger riders who simply lack a training plan.

Training like this has enabled me to race professionally for 10 years. During this upcoming race season, I know that I'll need a deep base of fitness. Training with Dave will allow me to develop this base. I can control the progression of my training loads with more accuracy by riding this way than I could mountain biking in the woods. And riding with Dave is more fun, anyway.

Dave's Training Log— Week 3

Date	Sleep/Wt.	Workout	Notes
Mon	8 hrs/16?		
Tue	9 hrs/16?	2 hrs: nice ride, easy pace	Sunny
Wed	8 hrs/168		
Thu	7 hrs/169	1 hr: moderate— 1? miles	Back is stiff
Fri	8 hrs/169		
Sat	9 hrs/168	2 hrs: great ride with Marla	Talked about training program and Century
Sun	8 hrs/168		

Total Riding Hours: **5**
Total Miles: **91**

Marla's Training Log— Week 3

Date	Sleep/Wt.	Workout	Notes
Mon	9 hrs/140	3 hrs: zones 2–3	Mtb ride with teammate; no balance or legs today, but fun trails
Tues	8 hrs/141		Off! (travel day)
Wed	11 hrs/142	1 hr: zones 1–2 Gym: 30 min— Upper body and back only Then rode moto for 30 min moderate pace	Rode easy to gym
Thu	8 hrs/141	1 hr run: zones 2–3	Moderate to brisk; walked up/down steep climbs
		30 min hike	To check trails; fell in river
Fri	5 hrs/140	1.5 hrs: zone 2	Easy road ride, checking out local real estate. Very tired.
Sat	6 hrs/139	2.5 hrs: zones 3–4	Nice ride with Dave; hit hills hard, with long recoveries; went over equipment stuff/bike fit
Sun	7 hrs/139	3 hrs: zone 2	Felt horrible, still not enough sleep

Total Hours: **12.5**

DAY 22 THROUGH 28 . . .
MOTIVATION—GETTING
OUT THE DOOR

CHAPTER
4

Getting out of bed in the morning is a killer. Some mornings the last thing I want to see is the probing nose of my saddle, stuck high in the air, as if saying in a bad De Niro impression, "What's a matter? You say sump'n, huh? You say sump'n ta me?"

I usually count my heartbeats until the clanging alarm silences itself. With armfuls of blankets, I cover my eyes from the morning light beaming off the top tube of my bike. In the darkness and under the quiet, I deny the morning. Whereas Marc rises in complete thoughts, speaking whole sentences and smiling, I cannot.

I'm grateful that Marc is very nonjudgmental and probably much happier embracing his morning undisturbed. He pulls on some shorts and a sweatshirt, slips into his Uggs, and then slides the wooden hatch and climbs the three steps of the ladder out into the world. He is so nimble that he can be out the door before the alarm's bells change the tone of their peal. When I know that I have to get out of bed, the last thing I want is Marc telling me that I should be getting out of bed.

Our boat, which is home for months at a time, is large and roomy as most boats go, but it is still not a house. The berth, more like a shelf, is more narrow than our bed at home. Nights tied to the dock are as fitful as the slapping rigging, lapping swells, and yapping birds. But the boat is really safe and a refuge in which to hide.

During the few morning moments that Marc leaves me to myself, I often wrestle the blankets. My legs are always achy in the morning. I wish I could crank them through one of those old-fashioned clothes ringers, bending and squeezing their length from big toe to midthigh over and over again until the knots and walnuts and ribbons of scars are once again soft and pliable, their stiff ache liberated by the pain of simple movement. "I don't have to do this," my mind whines. "It's cold outside." I send out a toe from under the warm blankets to confirm that it is indeed cold. And, of course, damp. I drop my foot to the chilly plywood of the cabin sole and flop around until I get a toehold on the Mexican floor rug. "Ughh. And it's a weekday, so there'll be a lot of car traffic."

I raise myself up on one elbow gingerly and peek out from under my hood of blankets through the thick round glass of the porthole. From a few inches above the waterline the view is limited to the shadows that ripple darkly around the wooden pilings of the dock against which we have been gently rubbing all night. I can tell by the mussels and seaweed low-water line on the old wooden pilings if the tide is high or low. "Okay, it won't be that cold. At least I don't need a skull cap and booties." Turning away from the porthole, I face amidships and the blankets fall from my shoulders while I take a stretch and sit upright. Arms out wide and long, snaps and pops from my spine, my eyes close tight with a moment of dizziness and the top of my head just whispers beneath the overhead of our berth. The yeasty sweet smell of warm, fresh bread from the hugely industrial H&S Bakery a few blocks away wafts through the boat's open deck hatches. Across the cabin a few inches above my bike, through the starboard portholes the bright colors of the promising dawn recede row after row into the gray mortar and iron brick of Fells Point.

On this boat, there is no such thing as a hot shower. Instead, I steady myself with one hand on the galley countertop and with my bare foot pump a floor lever, which juts out from beneath the cabinet of the galley sink, until cold, bracing water spurts from the faucet. As I splash water on my face and brush my teeth, if I can feel individual strands of my thigh's muscle as sharply defined as if they were rows of corduroy, then I know my ride might be difficult. But I'm up now and awake, so I should dress and prepare to ride anyway. I light the stove burner and set on it the heavily dented pot with the loose handle that we use to boil water for coffee.

Today, according to the training plan, is an "on" day. There is no way to be unaware of that. Every fiber of muscle in my legs is firing with the reminders that yesterday was easy and today won't be. I don't know which is more difficult: getting up for the first hard ride of the season, or one of the last rides when I'm worn and torn by the summer's end. This morning, I'll be riding not at Dave's pace, but my own. And unfortunately all alone. I haven't been living here in Baltimore long enough to hook up with some reliable roadies. Still seminaked, I stack on the bench a clean riding kit, my latest favorite Oakleys, my iPod, and a stick of gum. I stuff a Red Bull and a mint chocolate chip Clif Bar into the pockets on the back of my shell. Today I'll be riding for about 3 hours, so I plug in my iPod to make sure it has a full charge. All these rituals have been ingrained over the last 10 years and help me robotically get in the zone. By the time I finish dressing, there's no way of backing out.

Just as the water begins to boil over, Marc slides the hatch open. In he comes with the paper, the bright sunlight spilling down the stairs and, tumbling after, the honking horns of cars and the drone of their radials from Boston Street's morning traffic. He takes over in the galley pressing the coffee and dropping a handful of eggs into the remaining water in the pot to boil. He slices up a couple of bagels and pops them under the broiler. He cuts a grapefruit in half and sets each on two small plates, even though I've told him plenty of times that the coffee will strip out the grapefruit's vitamins before digestion. Then he flips a couple of switches and presses a bank of buttons, and the speakers crackle and chirp with morning news from the local NPR affiliate.

I slide onto the banquette on my side of the kitchen table and wait to be served. Even though my ride is already spelled out for me in my training plan, I reserve the right to make a final decision. After breakfast, though. Maybe I should just ride to the Kinko's on Charles Street and take care of some business that I've been shirking. I could always ride out on Old Harford Road and visit my mom and dad. There are a lot of things I could do besides follow my training program for the day. I could crack open that Web site software that sits on the shelf tightly shrunk-wrapped from the day I bought it a year ago. The coffee and newspaper help my brain evolve back up to at least the latest millennium. Without the caffeine, I wouldn't even bother trying to decipher the newspaper.

"Inside or out?" Marc wants to know.

"Inside's good. I'll be out in those elements soon enough."

I set the newspaper aside and open up my training plan notebook and pull my map from its last pages. The map's creases and folds are so thin that as I open it up on the table, I have to be as careful as though I were moving a jigsaw puzzle by its corners. Then I set the notebook open to today's page on top of my map. I quickly fill in the open cell under the heading Morning Heartbeat—45 beats per minute (BPM). Then my morning weight—140 pounds. I leave unmarked for now the cell where I intend to mark down what I will have eaten for breakfast and instead focus on the cell where today's ride is outlined. Then I psych myself up to fill in that sucker with something that will be noteworthy afterward. Something that'll blow my notebook's 3-ringed mind. If it had one.

Self-Help

There are really only a few people in the world who do exactly as they want, when and where and how. Children under the age of 4 for example. Rap stars and the Dahlai Lama. The rest of us do those things that we have to do pretty much from some sense of fear.

We go to work from fear of losing that job if we take the day off. We file our taxes because we know what will happen if we don't. Everyone fears the IRS.

As a pro rider, I'm terrified by the possibility that if I slack off for a day, my competition will get a leg up on me. Maybe you think the same. Or that you should ride lest your bad HDL will creep up and you'll drop from a heart attack, or that you'll never be able to fit into that Donna Karan pencil skirt that you just bought. Perhaps you'll get your ride in because you're terrified of the ragging that your riding buddies will give you if you miss the group ride. Maybe you're afraid of looking at yourself in the mirror that night as you brush your teeth before bed, knowing that you didn't make your ride that day. Fear can be a big motivator for getting on your bike, but I don't think it's the best.

Fear works. No doubt. You might be thinking there are more positive motivators out there, like guilt and remorse. But better still are a road map and your training plan, and the mantra, "I'm going for a bike ride this morning! Yes!" You gotta say that to yourself a few times until its meaning makes you smile: a bike ride. It's healthier to be positive. If it's cold and miserable out there, I assure myself that I'll feel great and vindicated once I start sweating. I tell myself once again, the hardest part is getting out the door.

This is not a robotic step class, one-two, one-two, up-down, up-down, in some expensive sweat club. This is a bike ride. Freedom. And speed. And the outside with its shapes and colors, smells and sounds that give rise to the thoughts, observations, and amusements on the inside. So real you can choke on it if a wet bug smacks you in the teeth. Spread that road map out. See on which roads you have chugged along before in a car, and choose one to take now by bike, and expect to be surprised by the difference. On your road of choice in a car, the only part of you that's alive might be your ears filled to the brims of your pinnas with the cacophony of the radio. In the car, you shuffle your zombie feet a little bit. One hand is dead on the wheel and the other crawls around looking for something to do while the world whizzes past on the other side of the safety glass. The only time your heart jumps a beat is when a jolt of spilled hot coffee galvanizes your lap like a bolt of electricity zapping some dead frog's legs. On your bike, this is a different road. The power plant of your own body is building this road with each pedal stroke. This road can take you through a world that is not artificial, or a shadow, but a world that is made live by the exertions of your own creation.

What is the plan for today? A 30-mile loop? Some sustained efforts, maybe in duration longer than any ride to date? Maybe you'll be a little late for work, but as long as you get your stuff done by the end of the day, who cares. There will be some pain, some heavy breathing, but you are on a bike. Stare at the check mark and exclamation points just beside yesterday's training ride. And the check mark beside the day before that, and so on all the way to Day 1. You want to give yourself another check mark, don't you? A gold star for today? Don't you?

Even though I'm a pro and despite being paid to ride, I don't ride because I get paid. I ride my bike because it's the best part of every day. Sometimes even a pro can lose track of that; that's why I know it can be even easier for a guy like Dave to stay in bed longer than he'd like to.

There are a couple of other tricks to get you out of bed and onto your bike in the right frame of mind.

The Partner Plan

If you're sharing a bed with someone, you need to have their support if you hope to stick with a 100-Day Training Plan for a Century

Ride. Good luck trying to hide anything for 100 days from the person with whom you share a bathroom. Give up or put up whatever you have to to win that support. I am lucky to have Marc. He's lucky I let him have a piddly little job as my manager, where he gets to hang out in coffee shops all day.

Enlisting the aid of your partner can be another whole book. But let's face it, if one wakes early, that means the other is waking early, too. Maybe not happily. You have to keep that in mind. If your training means a change in your eating habits, it's so much easier if your partner also adopts the new menu. If that long weekend ride requires the support of your partner in the family sag wagon, you better be prepared to return the favor with a dinner and a movie afterward.

In a perfect world, the person who shared your bed would also share your Century Riding lifestyle. And your partner may, but not necessarily to the same degree. But more likely, you will be the only one in your house training for a Century. Be positive that down the road, that may change as your craziness becomes catching. The world is largely imperfect, and even if you both ride, one is likely stronger or faster. One might have a lighter load at work, making it easier to put in the time on the bike. You may be able to squeeze in your riding in the morning, your partner during the afternoons.

If you're training solo for a Century with the blessing of your better half, you may find that the daily give-and-take on the small scale isn't sufficient. Consider a give-and-take on the large scale. That's basically the arrangement that Marc and I have come to. He supports my little happy bike riding, and I support his sailing, where we have to hand-steer in the cold rain for miles over long passages.

Some Little Tricks

Whatever arrangements your household has agreed upon in theory, there will be some practicalities that will have to be worked out. Getting out of bed is just the first step.

It's All Downhill after Getting Out of Bed

If you're the one for whom the early morning alarm bell tolls, try placing the alarm clock so that it's physically out of arm's reach. Like on top of a dresser on the other side of the room, so that in order to shut it off, you have to climb out of bed and walk a few steps. I find the best kind of alarm is the old-fashioned windup mechanical type, with the two bells on top and the gonging striker. I keep my clock in the sink, and the ring echoes out like a blaring fire engine doing donuts inside my head. The only way to shut it off is to get out of bed, stumble over to the sink, and flail around at the bottom until I can strangle the clock into submission. Then I splash my face with water until I become a civilized person again.

Trip Over Your Stuff

Another motivating trick is the strategic prepositioning of my bike. At night I display my bike in a prominent place, so that once I'm awake, I cannot pretend that I don't know I have one. Confronting my prepped and shiny bike first thing in the morning is a big hint that I'm supposed to ride it. I tried leaning it right against the bathroom door, but I didn't consider what would happen in the middle of the night. Marc is a very supportive partner and he said his bruises would heal quickly, but I have since found a more strategic location for my bike alongside the wall right opposite the bed.

The Bathroom Mirror

The bathroom is well known as a place where we confront the naked truths. Since we all have to deal with the harsh reality of the bathroom scale at some point during the day, take the opportunity for a little self-motivation. Hang a poster of someone you emulate like Floyd Landis, or pin a Polaroid of someone you *detestulate* like that guy on the Merlin who's always decked out in that Motorola kit and only takes pulls during the last half hour of the group ride. You can also motivate yourself with this morning's weight compared to yesterday's, by scribbling any change onto a corner of the mirror with a grease pen. Use the mirror. Talk to it while you chew your morning multivitamins. "Today, I am going to be a monster." Make muscles, suck in your gut, and admire the powerful cyclist that you see in the mirror. It sounds silly but it works. I don't use the mirror as a motivator as much as Marc does: When he's training for one of his semi-annual personal goals he sticks a small square mirror on the floor. He has the mirror set at such an angle that he can admire his calves as he brushes his teeth.

A friend of mine uses a supermodel calendar as motivation. He only allows himself to turn to the next month when he has finished all his workouts. I've seen him hammering a climb, telling me he wants to get to Miss September. Whatever works is less crazy than simply not trying.

Cycling Is Inherently a Social Pursuit

As far as motivation, your life partner can help with encouragement, but added pressure from that person is not recommended. It's very tricky business. The line between the support from someone you love and pressure from someone you love is a line you don't want to ever be near. But peer pressure is too powerful a prod to leave unutilized. In a later chapter, I'll provide some tips on how to actually latch on to group rides, but for now just keep in mind that riding with a peloton of buddies will probably be the single most significant motivator for riding a Century.

Road riding is easier with a group. Physically, that is. The greatest effort a cyclist makes is not the energy transfer between muscle exertion and the drivetrain's forward inertia. The largest obstacle to overcome is not the rider's strength-to-weight ratio, although a high ratio is handy on steep climbs. A cyclist's biggest battle is with an adversary that most everyone would agree is so minute as to be invisible, so weightless as to have no mass, so universal as to be forgotten: air. A rider puts out 30 percent less effort when drafting, which is sticking to someone else's wheel.

A peloton primarily fights air pressure better than a solo rider. A riding group puts on its own kind of pressure as well. The peloton exerts a primal pressure immeasurable beyond any scale of foot-pounds. All peer groups do. The power of peer pressure was exacting enough to convince you to get that tribal tattoo on your ankle, persuade you to pierce your nose, or cajole you into going out on that disastrous blind date. But enlistment of peer pressure to motivate you onto your bike is a shrewd move. You'll find yourself scrambling to be on time for the start of a group ride solely because you told some people that you'd show.

The psychology of why peer pressure works can be reduced to two terms: shame and pride. If you have committed yourself to riding with a couple of others, you'll find it almost impossible to avoid them forever if you have shamefully dodged them once. They will hunt you down now that you have revealed a weakness and they want to exert their dominance over you. Your riding buddies with whom you may share mutual friends, common political opinions, educational backgrounds, and a keen appreciation for the finer coffee concoctions are actually a pack of feral dogs. There is the alpha and then a squabbling, jostling, striving hierarchy of everybody else. The exhilaration of pride that you'll feel on the friendly Saturday morning ride when your group works as a team to drop your best friend knows no bounds. You'll see. Group rides are more fun than you can imagine.

Dave's Training Log— Week 4

Date	Sleep/Wt.	Workout	Notes
Mon	8 hrs/168		
Tue	9 hrs/166	1 hr: easy	Had trouble getting motivated in light rain
Wed	8 hrs/168		
Thu	7 hrs/169	30 min: easy spin	Pretended I was a pro
Fri	8 hrs/169	1.5 hrs: easy to moderate up climbs	Back still sore; 24 miles
Sat	7 hrs/170		
Sun	8 hrs/169	1 hr	Almost didn't ride today, but Marla talked me into it; cold and windy

Total Riding Hours: **4**
Total Miles: **68**

Marla's Training Log— Week 4

Date	Sleep/Wt.	Workout	Notes
Mon	7 hrs/139	2.5 hrs: zones 2–3 mtb	Photo shoot; hard day with lots of pushing up hills, hitting scary jumps, and posing
Tue	8 hrs/141	30 min spin (then travel day)	Tired and sore
Wed	9 hrs/141	2 hrs: zones 2–4	Preran race course; felt good, nice day (3x5 min seated efforts); new bike!
Thu	2 hrs/140	2 hrs: zones 2–3	Testing bikes; some quick jumps with other racers; 45 min cooldown
Fri	8 hrs/140	2 hrs: zone 2	Very easy road ride to recover for race; still testing equipment— titanium bike fits well
Sat	9 hrs/139	2 hrs: zones 3–4	Long day with lots of media stuff; rode well, got 5th in crit; legs fried
Sun	7 hrs/139	1.5 hrs: zones 3–5	Crashed on 3rd turn, but re-covered, bridged, and came up to front to end up on the podium (4th); no cooldown

Total Hours: **12.5**

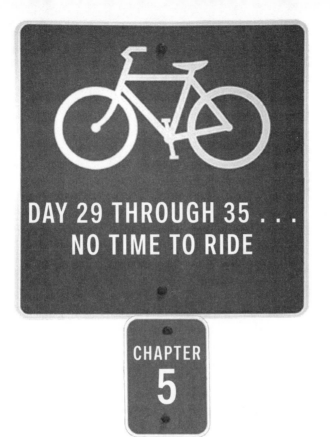

DAY 29 THROUGH 35 . . . NO TIME TO RIDE

CHAPTER 5

"There's no way I'll be able to ride today. I'm not even sure I can ride this week. I'm just swamped with work." Dave sounded genuinely distressed. Almost embarrassed, as if it were somehow his fault or a slight against his character that he couldn't go for a bike ride.

"Don't worry about that. You can try to make up today's ride tomorrow."

"It doesn't look like I'll be anywhere but this desk for a few days."

"Oh, just go for a run or something. When you can squeeze it in. Just an hour. When you're downloading something, or waiting for your hard drive thingy to uninstall or whatever it does."

Dave ignored my suggestion. Instead he just went on about how he wasn't sticking with his plan. "What's the point of even trying when I won't be able to stick with it? The boys have an overnight scouting trip this week. Lorena is talking about fixing up the garage as a studio space. She really needs it. A bike ride is just the farthest thing down on the list."

"Think of it this way, Dave. If you don't work, you won't be able to afford to ride your bike anyway. So working is as much a part of your cycling plan as anything else. Your wife and kids are the most important things in your life. You'll always be there for them. But they also want you to do this Century thing. You know that, don't you? So just do some situps and pushups and call that your workout. And be glad about it. You're doing a great job!"

"You certainly do a pretty good job of justifying things, Marla. Putting a positive spin on stuff."

"Yes, well you know that comes from experience."

"You're so good I'm surprised you ride at all."

"That's not it. Believe me, I love riding my bike, but sometimes it's just not going to happen. I've found it's much better to deal with truth in a realistic manner."

"You don't feel bad about it? About not doing your ride?"

"I feel great that I went to the gym for a half hour instead."

"Hmmph."

"Okay then. I'll check back with you about the weekend. It's supposed to be warm . . . "

"Okay. Talk to you then. And thanks."

"No problem," I said. How would I know? I'm not married. I don't have any kids. I'm not trying to run my own business. As I was heading out the door for my own ride, the only comforting thought I could squeeze from my own conscience about cajoling him into this bike riding stuff was that he really does love it. And that I love him for trying.

No time to ride? Who has time to ride? Nobody, really. The way to deal with the reality that life is full of stuff that has priority over riding a bicycle is to accept that some compromises will have to be made. In other words, cheat.

Say it's late in the afternoon, and your printer is still not on speaking terms with your PC, and the sun will have sunk below the horizon in less than an hour. Just the thought of attempting to sneak in a ride makes you anxious. The image of ripping a gaping hole in your training diary makes you feel guilty. There is no way a real ride is going to happen today. But you can still cheat.

During the first few weeks of your training, you will invariably have come across a hill or two. And now that drab hillock, that subtle drumlin, is going to save your day. Even a multistory parking garage can work in a pinch to keep you on your Century training plan. All you need is just an hour.

Hill Repeats

One hour. That's all. Including a warmup and a cooldown, from start to finish, from training plan ruination to training plan vindication. That hill near work or close to the house that has at least a minute of climbing is all you need. If you live in Kansas or Florida, the tensioner on the stationary trainer at the gym will do. Use the 15-minute ride en route to the hill's base to warm up. If you find that you're driving to your hill, remember, you still have to warm up on your bike. Even though the duration of this workout will be comparatively short, warming up is a must. This will be an intense ride, and you don't want to pull a muscle. So, get out of the car, unload your bike, and ride around the block for 15 minutes. If possible, leave the car at work.

Warmup: You want to get the blood flowing, open up the lungs, and kink out those joints. A sheen of light sweat across your brow is a good sign that you're warmed up. After this 15 minutes of easy spinning, roll up to the hill in a gear that you can spin comfortably near 80 rpm. Now you're ready. A hill repeat is comprised of two elements: the hill part and the repeat part.

The hill part: The grade of the hill does not have to be a gut-busting, granny-gear climb, but it must be steep enough that you cannot maintain your optimum cadence of between 80 to 100 rpm in your favorite flat-road gear. The hill should have at least a 5 percent grade. Depending on the hill's size, you can ride it all from base to summit, ride from the bottom partway to the top, or start halfway up and ride to the crest. Whichever part of the hill you choose to attack, climb for 3 minutes in zone 4, finishing in zone 5 at the top.

Ideally, you want to ride so hard that you think you will throw up. Now that's a good effort. Then you turn around. Pretty simple, huh?

Each hill repeat can last from 1 to 10 minutes. There is no shame in petering out after only a minute or so. After all, we're simply saving your training plan from total abandonment. For our purposes, you want to ride to the point of failure and then recover quickly. The hill repeat workout is as much about learning how to recover from a big effort as training in order to make those big efforts.

Note your start and end points by choosing a landmark like a fence post or sewer grate, so that your climbs will be consistent. During your climb, check your heart rate if you're wearing a monitor. If you're not, just try to be aware of how hard your carotid artery is straining against your shirt collar. The last few seconds of your hill repeat, don't be surprised if you see angels, feel bathed in a warm white light from the end of a tunnel, or imagine the smell of your mom's Toll House cookies fresh from the oven. While you roll back down, keep spinning to flush out your legs. During your recovery, after you find your lungs again, you can pretend none of that ever happened. Live in that moment of accomplishment. Relish the short time of rest. At the bottom, roll around in a couple of figure eights until your heart rate drops back down and your breathing returns to normal levels. This should only take a minute or two.

The repeat part: It should be harder than the hill part. You really want to make it difficult for yourself. It's only a few minutes. I often trick myself by saying "only one more time." I find this easier psychologically.

Eight repeats is a nice round number to shoot for. If it's not that difficult the second time, don't worry. The third and fourth and so on will become harder than high school ever was. Your form will fracture.

Your cadence will crumble. Dizziness, nausea, and cramping in the quadriceps are all common experiences. All this from just a little hill and a few minute's effort.

Trick yourself into believing that you're not climbing at all. You're on flat ground; try to ride that way. Don't worry, you won't be able to, you are after all on a hill. But what works well on the flats—high cadence, pedaling circles, flat back, hands on the hoods—can work even better on a hill. And similarly, any bad habits that you already have on flat pavement are exaggerated on a grade. Occasionally standing will relieve certain muscle groups, and disappoint other ones.

Remember to breathe. And smile. A lot of people are so determined to make such a heroic hill effort that they actually forget to breathe for the first few seconds of their climb. That's not the best strategy. You'll see the angels much sooner than you should that way.

Try not to squeeze your bar grips. Bulging forearms do look cool, but the effort is a waste of energy. Your grip should be finger light, the triceps and biceps as relaxed as possible. Relaxing your shoulders and going easy on the grips is harder to accomplish than you might think. Imagine that the wall thickness of the bar's tubing is as thin as an eggshell. Your body weight should be on your pedals and the horn of your saddle, not propped up on your elbows.

When standing, pull up on the handlebar slightly to counter your pedal stroke. That creates a gentle rocking motion and is a very efficient way to maximize your output. This usually happens naturally.

Climbing in this controlled manner may not seem that macho. You might think it better to torque your way up the grade, your bottom bracket flexing a few inches and your head tube twisting like licorice while your nostrils snort and flare like a bull. You might. It is more macho to lock the major muscle groups in a titanic effort of tetanus, but not as fast as learning how to spin. Singlespeeders have no choice, but if you have a derailleur on your bike, then these hill repeats are as much about *form* as per*form*ance. Learning how to do hill repeats this way enables you to do the repeat part of the hill repeat. The gnarly

David Smith

Out of the saddle, on the hills.

macho mashers who grind themselves up the hill usually can't get back up again, and how macho is that? Same with those frenetic fems. They'll also be finished.

Quick circles will be hard to scribe, but worth the effort if you can stay on top of your gear as best you can. Climbing this way will look easy to everybody else on the road. But it's not. You will need a lot of core strength to suspend the pedals from your feet. You will be concentrating so hard on making circles that you'll forget to breathe. And so, maintaining steady breathing becomes just one more work effort that's invisible to any onlooker. But the big effort will be emanating from your quadriceps and glutes. Those thighs and hamstrings and calf muscles will swell up right under your clothes. The hydraulic pressure from all that blood rushing into those muscles will test the seams of your clothing's fabric.

During hill repeats, your cadence might collapse as you climb; that's the idea. Be careful with your shifting, concentrate on smooth power circles, and alternate between being seated and standing. Repeatedly working yourself to failure while striving to maintain good form during hill repeats is not just sadomasochism. Working to failure quickly builds muscle while teaching you when and how to recognize the upper end of your performance range. The work is trying to forestall the failure point as long as possible, and in doing so, become stronger.

Watch the Outdoor Living Network (OLN) coverage of the Tour de France during the big climbs. Check out the fastest climbers in the world—high cadence, relaxed upper body, dropped elbows, minimal sway, regular breathing. In the pro peloton, the riders with the worst form during the great climbs are either just about to be pulled or are wearing the polka dot jersey as the stage winner.

If your hill is the right size so that you can actually crest it within your interval, be sure to climb right over the summit. You won't understand how easy it is to convince yourself that you're at the top when you actually have a ways to go. Stay on top of your gear, and crank over the peak's plateau, and shift through your cog set. Working over the top like that has to be fired into your brain and muscle memory in order to actually be able to do it under eventlike conditions. In races, I have fought all the way up the climb only to lose my lead at the summit by not attacking all the way over the top. Preventing that is not just a matter of willpower; your body must continue to climb over the top like an autonomic reflex, like a chicken running around with its head cut off. Well, maybe not like that.

Even if you promise yourself that your Century Ride will be strictly a fun ride, you eventually might find yourself racing. You'll want to climb the hills that way, or pull away on the flats. That's what happens when a bunch of people hop on bicycles. Racing happens to messengers, newspaper deliverers, and Century Riders.

A computer can be really helpful during hill repeats. The time it took to reach your fence post on the first climb may be different than on the fifth climb. Don't be surprised if the time to cover the same distance doubles. Just hang in there.

If your form on the climbs is really deteriorating, or if you're becoming so fatigued as you crank up the hill that you can't get your heart rate up, take more recovery time at the bottom. Try a 1:3 ratio of effort to recovery. Spin down the street for a couple of minutes until your breathing resumes a more normal level. Don't worry; you aren't bonking. You're just in mid-recovery. Take a pull from your water bottle, breathe deep a couple more times, and then climb the hill again.

A 15-minute warmup, then a workout of ten 1-minute hill climbs, or five 3-minute hill climbs with recovery, and then finishing with a 15-minute cooldown should take about an hour.

Then, you'll want a massage. Or if you're home alone, you can just elevate your legs.

Hill repeats on a day when you don't have much time to ride can really save the day and keep you on your training plan. When you get back home and put your legs up, take a moment and amend your training plan. Cross out what you had planned for a ride and write down what you actually did for a ride. And then gloat.

I usually don't include formal hill repeats in my training plan like I would a high-mileage workout, a high-intensity session, or a recovery ride. Instead, I have learned that life interrupts my formal training plans frequently enough that hill repeats become the default workout. To paraphrase the bumper sticker, Hill Repeats Happen. I don't plan on doing hill repeats, because they are always there for me. Flipping through the training diaries from seasons past proves that hill repeats are a great way to cheat.

But there are occasions when even hill repeats aren't possible. Inclement weather or fatigue will probably be the main reasons why you'll have to cheat on your 100-Day Training Plan. But there will be plenty of other reasons why you find you cannot get away for a bike ride. What to do then? Here are more alternatives, but the possibilities are endless. Use your imagination when cheating.

Floor exercises—stretching, pushups, situps

Gym time

Spin sessions on a stationary trainer

Running, hiking, and ditch digging

A quick ride around town on errands

Floor Exercises

Floor exercises are a great way to make the best out of a bad situation. I'm not talking about lying on the carpet for an hour while you watch Oprah or the Big Game on TV with a fluffy pillow beneath your head. I'm talking about a real effort.

Stretching, pushups, and situps should be a part of everybody's daily routine like brushing your teeth, or drinking eight glasses of water. I'm sure we all brush, but how many of us really drink the eight glasses . . . that's a lot of water. Even fewer of us do the basic stretches throughout the day. There are dozens of illustrated books available that outline the more advanced stretching techniques. A daily floor routine with an exercise ball can be squeezed into 10 or 15 minutes. If that's not possible, try stretching for 20 minutes on those off days that are set aside in your training plan.

You probably feel pretty harried just squeezing in the time for a bike ride, so stretching is dispensed with. That's okay. Today you find that you just can't ride. Not even hill repeats. Can't even touch your bike. But you can certainly stretch. The last resort is the occasional 1-hour stretch session when there's no time to ride.

I know that I should stretch daily. The reality is that I consistently find the time on a daily basis for a few weeks, and then for one reason or another, I trail off. However, I often find myself with 2-hour layovers at airports. That's a perfect time to stretch. Travel itself can be exhausting. It is very rare that I'm able to ride my bike on a travel day. After an airport shuttle, baggage check, security hassles, delays, baggage pickup, car rental, and hotel check-in, a solid stretching session is the best I could hope for. If you find yourself stretching in an airport terminal or an empty conference room at work, just block out the incredulous stares of passersby. The security guard will eventually signal when it's time for you to cool down.

Cheating with a stretching or yoga session accomplishes a couple of goals. The primary reason for stretching is the benefit of the exercise itself: increased circulation, range of motion, overall body awareness, muscle recovery, deep breathing, and overall stress reduction. But just as important, and where the cheating really evidences itself, is the opportunity to write down in your training plan, "stretched 1 hour, hamstrings still too tight, and lower back tender," rather than striking a black line through the planned ride for that day, rending a gaping hole in your training plan. Stretching can keep you on track. And stretching can clue you in to how your body is holding up to the demands of your riding.

There are seven basic stretches that I find a cyclist can really benefit from. They are shown on pages 65 to 67.

1. Hamstring stretch

2. Neck roll

3. Calf, Achilles tendon, and plantar fascia stretch

4. Quadriceps stretch

5. Trunk twist

6. Forearm stretch

7. Toe touch

Hamstring Stretch

Neck Roll

Calf, Achilles Tendon, and Plantar Fascia Stretch

Quadriceps Stretch

TRUNK TWIST

FOREARM STRETCH

Toe Touch

Try to perform all seven by gently holding each stretch without bouncing for at least 20 seconds. You want to smooth over those swollen fibers, stretch out that kinky connective tissue. Close your eyes, inhale, deeply exhale, and reach slowly for a deeper stretch. Relax. Then stretch again, holding for 30 seconds. Each deep exhalation should enable further relaxation and a fuller stretch. You should immediately see a slight improvement in your range of motion, a tiny increase in your extent of flexibility. You'll feel sinews whose names you don't know, and there may be some noises like snapping bubble wrap, but there should be no pain. Pain is not an objective here. After an intense stretching session, you might even feel the tingly glow of fatigue that you expect from a light ride, but never any lingering soreness. Being slightly out of breath and a few drops of perspiration are good signs that your stretching sessions are doing some good. As your cycling workouts build your muscle, a stretching regimen protects them. None of us is as resilient as we were in our youth, so flexibility, range of motion, and joint expression are factors that we have to be mindful of. Now that you're all limbered up, you can throw in some situps, pushups, leg raises, and other exercises that build up your core.

Gym Time

I used to hate the gym. I imagine many cyclists do. Cyclists are typically skinny, with strange tan lines, and generally not thrilled about the prospect of working out indoors. Exercising in a gym always makes me feel gypped that I'm not outside breathing in some fresh air, dodging a few ground squirrels, and soaking up the vitamin D. It's hard to measure up against the gym rats with their big "guns," tanning booth whole-body tans, and loud grunting. Yet the gym can be an attractive workout alternative when you're really pressed for time, when the weather is beating you down, or if you're beat up with an injury.

There are many instances when a gym makes a lot more logistical sense than a bike ride, e.g., your downtown office is across the street from 24 Hour Fitness. Try as you might, I have found that you can't live in a cycling bubble . . . for very long. Once or twice a week during the winter season, I'll squeeze in a quick ride downtown to a gym, pay the drop-in fee—usually less than 10 bucks—sneak in a weight session, and afterward Marc will swing by in our VW with a bag of girl clothes so he can take me to dinner and a movie.

Over the years, I've found that the great outdoors is not the best place to be working out when it's raining and snowing and pitch-black at 3:00 in the afternoon. Initially, I fought Mother Nature with studded tires on my mountain bike, multilayers of fleece and neoprene, and NiCad battery packs for my bike lights, but I now sign up for a local gym membership when I begin to notice Halloween decorations in the front yards as I ride past.

If I find myself slipping into the gym on a rainy winter afternoon to sneak in a workout, I make the most of the occasion by working on muscle groups that complement, rather than supplant, my normal training rides. If I know that I will be spending the next 2 months in the weight room instead of on my bike, I plan my workouts accordingly. For instance, if I've been riding regularly, and I'm only in the gym today because it's sleeting and snowing, I'm not going to lift heavy weights with my legs. My legs are already getting a good workout on the bike. It's only in the winter or early preseason that I work on legs.

But so much time on the bike can cannibalize the musculature of the shoulders, upper arms, and back, so now that I've snuck into the gym, those are the muscle groups that I train. There is always temptation to work on your strengths rather than your weaknesses. I know it would give my ego a great boost to saunter over to the squat rack, load up the bar with a few of the largest 45-pound plates, and squat the big guys to shame, but how does that benefit my cycling? Well, it doesn't during the season. I probably wouldn't be able to ride worth a damn the next couple of days when the weather clears. It's a bit embarrassing to tiptoe over to the small side of the dumbbell rack and slink off with two 15-pound weights to do puny biceps curls. But that does help my cycling. So do the wheezing chinups, the red-faced bench presses, the doddering dead lifts, the trembling back extensions, the slouching shoulder shrugs, and the ungainly military presses. These muscle groups—the deltoids, lats, pecs—must balance out the calf, thigh, hamstring, and butt muscles that my bike has been taking care of.

To work on these muscle groups, you don't have to belong to a fancy gym or know all the names of the muscle groups displayed on the four-color anatomical rendering hanging above the gym's water fountain. You can get a great workout on a basic Universal Machine, which can be found at almost any high school or health club. Or you can lift weights the old-fashioned way . . . with dumbbells in each hand and some barbell presses. One thing to keep in mind is that gym time is not necessarily training time. It is really easy to lose yourself in a gym's wall of cable televisions, floor-to-ceiling mirrors, juice bar pickup scene, and jazzercise arenas for hours at a stretch. So you should promise yourself that you'll get your workout done in 45 minutes. That's 45 minutes, in and out, with a quick shower thrown in. There are a few basic lifting exercises to start with.

Strength Workout—Quick and Easy

After warming up with some cardio and stretching, start these quick exercises to enhance and strengthen your cycling performance. Keep a log of your workout, including weights, sets, and reps. Add weight when reps become too easy. Most of these can be done at home.

CRUNCH—*3 sets of 30 (for abdominals)*

1. Lie on your back with bent knees, put your hands behind your head or on your chest, and curl your shoulders off the floor about 8 inches.

2. Concentrate on pulling your belly button toward your spine.

3. Go SLOW, and repeat until you feel the burn.

4. Crunches are even better on a medicine ball.

BACK EXTENSION—*3 sets of 20 (for lower back)*

1. Use the back extension stand in the gym or lie down on the floor face down. Contract your lower back muscles to lift your torso.

2. Cross your arms over your chest or add a weight to add resistance.

3. Go SLOW and exhale during the contraction.

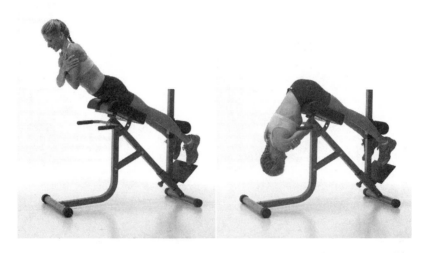

SQUAT OR LEG PRESS—*3 sets of 15 (for quads, glutes, and back)*

1. Use a light weight to start—don't overdo it!

2. Always use a spotter or safety rack to catch the bar.

3. Keeping your feet flat, head up, and back straight, hold the bar on your shoulders and slowly bend your knees until your thighs are parallel with the floor. Watching a mirror helps with form.

4. Leg press machines also work well and may be easier on the knees, but don't lock them on the extension.

5. Repeat until you feel a burn in your thighs.

BENCH PRESS—*3 sets of 12 (for chest, shoulders, and triceps)*

1. Use a light weight to start and a spotter.

2. Lie on a bench with your feet flat on the floor. Start with the bar on your chest slightly below nipple level and raise it up to full extension.

3. Go slowly and exhale during contraction.

4. Pushups can replace this exercise at home.

Strength Workout—Extras

Here are some more exercises if you have the time. These are also important for conditioning, stability, and strength on long rides.

LUNGE—*3 sets of 30 (for quads and glutes)*

1. Hold weights or a bar on your shoulders and step with one leg until the forward thigh is parallel to the floor.

2. Push back to standing and repeat with the other leg.

3. Adjust the amount of reps until your legs feel like rubber.

BENT-OVER ROW—*3 sets of 15 (for back extensors and deltoids)*

1. Using hand weights or a barbell, bend forward until your back is parallel to the floor. Keep your knees slightly bent.

2. Pull the weight up to your chest, keeping your hands shoulder-width apart, then lower them slowly. Keep your back straight.

3. Squeeze your shoulder blades together during this exercise.

HAMSTRING ROLL—*3 sets of 15 (for hamstrings and glutes)*

1. Lie on your back with your feet on the top of an exercise ball.

2. Lift your hips until your legs are parallel with your back.

3. Slowly roll the ball toward your butt, keeping your hips high. Roll the ball back slowly.

4. Try this exercise with one foot on the ball, keeping the other leg vertical. Alternate legs. Now that burns!

TRICEPS EXTENSION—*3 sets of 15 (for triceps)*

1. Hold a light barbell overhead, and slowly bend your elbows until the weight is behind your neck.

2. Lift the barbell back over your head, keeping your arms tucked near your ears.

3. This can also be done on a triceps machine, pulling the bar down from your shoulders to your thighs. Be sure to keep your elbows next to your rib cage.

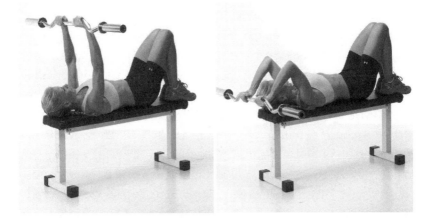

If you're in the gym more than twice a week because of bad riding weather or nurturing an injury, it's a good idea to mix up your weight lifting routine. The body adapts very well to stress, so if you always do the same kind of workout, your body will get used to it and your gains will decrease. There are plenty of resources on weight lifting: books, videos, and magazines. Some of the images can be intimidating, but comfort yourself with the knowledge that those behemoths may be able to move a mountain but are unlikely to be able to ride up one.

Spin Sessions on a Stationary Trainer

Even better than hack squats or calf raises is a 45-minute sweat session on one of the gym's stationary bikes. Don't be embarrassed while stuck on a stationary bike to ride like you're dropping the peloton. An MP3 player does a good job of allowing you to ignore the stares and guffaws of onlookers while you attempt your breakaway. I strongly recommend to the guys that while riding on a stationary bike in the gym, you avoid wearing your classic Banesto Lycra shorts. Make do in a T-shirt and a pair of gym shorts, and you'll suffer fewer incidences of stationary bike rage, a lesser known but just as hazardous analog to the more common road rage.

I've ridden rollers through many winters. I prefer my old set of Kreitler rollers to the newer stationary trainers that you mount your bike to. The rollers are simpler, cheaper, lighter, and help with pedaling technique. The stationary trainers are more widely available. They may cost a little bit more, but they offer a lot more gee-whiz stuff. The high-end models of trainers are integrated with heart rate monitors and cycle computers, and a few even hook up to the TV, which allows you to pretend that you're riding a beautiful country road as it scrolls past on the screen. I like my rollers because you actually have to ride . . . unlike on the stationary trainers on which you sort of just sit. You can't fall off or crash on a stationary trainer. But it's a personal preference.

Getting started on rollers, you'll need a sturdy wooden chair to set up beside you—helpful when clicking in. You can hold on to the back of the chair with one hand while you position the bike on the rollers and wobble on its saddle. Keep your hand on the chair while you clip in your feet and start to slowly spin. The first time you take your hand off the chair, it may be too soon. The first couple of times, actually.

Stopping comes more naturally, especially if you find yourself on the floor of the garage. Using the chair takes a little more practice, but it's essentially the reverse of getting started: Gently reach out your hand for the back of the chair, slow your cadence, unclick one foot, then the other, then gingerly set one foot onto the seat of the chair and you're done. You get a pretty good cardio workout just learning how to ride rollers.

I keep my rollers on the boat. Not just to show off to other bewildered boaters that I'm riding a bike on my boat's foredeck, but because the rollers are so portable, simple, and convenient to use that I can cheat in a quick ride even at anchor. That takes practice though, especially when the boat is rocking.

If any kind of riding is just impossible, then it's time for the Swedish ball, a sturdy chair, and lots of situps, pushups, and dips. But at least I can make an entry in my training log.

Hiking and Running

Hiking and running can be good alternatives if time does not allow you to follow your cycling plan for the day. It's also good for a change of pace. If your time for a workout is limited to 1 hour, you can still do a good job maintaining your cardio level of fitness through bipedal exercise. Try to mimic your cycling workouts as much as possible. If your plan calls for an easy day, brisk walking may be more appropriate than running. Try to hit your target intensity zones as called for in your plan. These workout alternatives may not do much to increase your technique, power, or speed on the bike, but they can be an effective way to stay on track with your plan.

The intensity of a run or hike can be increased by going up steep hills. Hills are always reliable like that. Another way to increase the cardio benefit is by swinging your arms and rotating your shoulders in an exaggerated manner. Keep an eye on your heart rate. Lift your knees high, set a high pace, and breathe deeply. Hiking up trails rather than down tends to have less of a negative impact on any chronic injuries that you may have. If you have knee problems, shin splints, or other issues, be careful and treat the way back down the trail as your cooldown. Even though you're not on the bike, carry a couple of water bottles with you. Hydrating is always a good idea, and the added weight increases your cardio load.

Running or jogging is a great way to sneak in a workout when you might not have time for or access to riding. Good footwear is the best way to prevent injury. Consider running on trails or on the grass beside a roadway, since the pavement can be much harder on your body. On irregular terrain, watch out for twisted ankles. Warm up for 15 to 30 minutes, run at a comfortable pace for about 30, and cool down for 15. If you're not used to running, ease into it with shorter runs for a few weeks. Because your cycling has given you a good cardio base, you could unknowingly run yourself right into the ground and develop nagging shin splints or muscle tears.

Dave's Training Log— Week 5

Date	Sleep/Wt.	Workout	Notes
Mon	9 hrs/168		
Tue	7 hrs/168	1 hr total: easy pace	Rode home from dropping kids off, then rode back to school to pick them up!
Wed	8 hrs/169		
Thu	8 hrs/168	1 hr: easy	Squeezed this ride in between meetings
Fri	7 hrs/167		
Sat	7 hrs/167	1.5 hrs: moderate to hard intensity	Fun session with Tom Dandy; tried to stay with him on the climbs
Sun	8 hrs/168		

Total Riding Hours: **3.5**
Total Miles: **58**

Marla's Training Log— Week 5

Date	Sleep/Wt.	Workout	Notes
Mon	6 hrs/139		Off (travel day)
Tue	12 hrs/141	2 hrs at zones 2–4 4x5 min standup hill repeats at zone 4 (30 min cooldown)	Felt great, finally; good energy
Wed	9 hrs/141	1.5 hrs: zones 2–4 2x10 min seated efforts at lower zone 4 30 min zone 2	Wrist is killing me Playing around on mtb
Thu	8 hrs/140	1 hr: zones 1–2 easy recovery ride 30 min run moderate pace	Felt fine
Fri	8 hrs/139	1.5 hrs: zone 2	Still trying to fit bike; didn't eat enough—bonked!
Sat	9 hrs/139	1 hr: zone 2	Hectic group ride; a few jumps to sprint for city signs
Sun	8 hrs/138	2 hrs: zone 4	Good warmup; felt great; stayed in front of group; flatted
Total Hours: **10**			

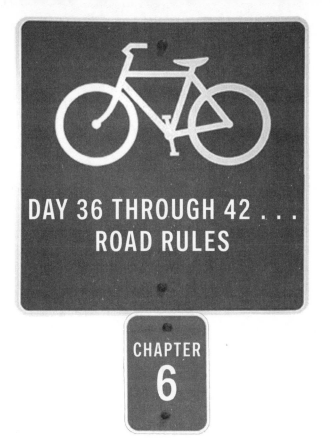

DAY 36 THROUGH 42 . . .
ROAD RULES

CHAPTER
6

The morning rain of winter's first real storm in Marin fell to the earth through oak trees denuded of leaves. Young saplings swooned over the redwood fences, and the old gnarled madrone trees began to totter over shingled rooftops as the soil, which had anchored their roots through so many previous storms, softened.

We had just moved up here to the San Francisco Bay area from San Diego, and such a severe storm was a surprise. As the afternoon whistled on, whole trees upended, snapping power lines. When I woke to the dark morning in my small apartment in Fairfax, there wasn't a sound. Not the drone of an automobile's wheels, not the hum of a refrigerator, not the blabbity-blabbing from a single TV. Except for the rhythmic blasts of Marc's snoring, it was as quiet as though I had submerged my head in a tub full of water. I curled up in bed waiting for the sun to rise and then nudged Marc awake. He crawled back into bed a few minutes later with a folded newspaper damp from the coin-op box down the hill. The power was going to be out for days in some places, the headlines of the *Marin Independent Journal* intoned.

We strolled through the puddle, twig-strewn, pinecone—littered town of Fairfax chatting with friends and neighbors, since none of us were in a rush to do anything until the waters receded and after the power came back on. By dinner time, there wasn't much left in the fridge that hadn't taken on a funky smell, and not one of the town's restaurants or either of its markets had opened, so Marc made omelets on the gas stovetop. Scrabble play by candlelight was a cheating scandal. When we fell asleep, the batteries in our radio were almost dead.

The next morning's *IJ* warned that the power outage extended north from Marin well into Sonoma, and beyond into Mendocino, with the coast taking the brunt of the storm's damage. It might be a week before we could use our coffee machine. Over a breakfast of cowboy coffee and plain oatmeal swimming in souring milk, Marc and I discussed our options. We could ride the half hour to Sausalito and then sail our little boat over to San Francisco for a couple of days where there was electricity and hot clam chowder in sourdough bread bowls at Pier 39, dim sum in Chinatown, or fiery chicken burritos in the Mission. We grew excited and quickly agreed that if we camped out in San Francisco until the power came back on in Fairfax, we would go broke. But we concluded that as long as we were sleeping in our cold-water apartment, we might as well load up our bikes and ride up the coast for a day or two. Camp out. See the redwoods. Watch for whales from the bluffs. Treat ourselves to a hot shower in a bed-and-breakfast when we got far enough north where there was power.

That morning as we pedaled out of town, we swerved around the bands of hide-and-seekers playing among the trunks of the toppled trees. Couples young and old walking hand in hand down the yellow center stripes waved and smiled. Cars remained sidelined along the curb. I promised Marc I'd ride easy. Once out of the valley, we had Highway One to ourselves since there is no city of any size along the coast north of San Francisco until you reach Eureka. This stretch of rolling highway, frothy blue ocean on one side, bovine-spotted hills on the other, is great bike riding under normal conditions. On this day, it was amazing. The only eye contact we made with others was with the blank stares of dairy cows that moved their heads in jerks from side to side as we pedaled past. We bought some cheese just past Point Reyes and a dozen oysters in Tomales, and when we skidded into Bodega Bay, we sat at the edge of a rickety wooden dock, our bike shoes dangling over the water, and pointed out to each other the whimsical names painted on the old wooden fishing trawlers that surrounded us. When we climbed back on our bikes and pedaled up the road, the air was still sweet with the brine of seaweed, waves, and fresh grass—not a whiff of car exhaust. We camped on the beach that night near the mouth of the Russian River in front of a smoky drift-wood fire.

The next morning further up the road, in an area the roadside signs proclaimed as the Lost Coast, the redwoods grew so impenetrable that Highway One turned inland, twisting and curving under the shadowy and damp cover of the old growth forest. The hooting of owls instead of the tooting of horns echoed through the woods. The road's shoulder diminished with time's passage until it withered into a bony narrow ribbon. We pedaled side by side, our handlebars almost touching, for long stretches.

Neither of us had been in a forest of giant trees before. The road's centerline faded and the highway devolved into one lane, the rare occasional cars avoiding head-ons with each other by swinging wildly into the dirt, kicking up gravel at the road's edge. As the afternoon warmed up, huge flatbeds lumbered out of the shadows, their approach muffled by the old growth's dew-laden air. A red flag the size of a handkerchief dangling from the logs front and rear, they swept the pebbles from the banks of the road's blind turns.

From a pay phone at a roadside gas station/coffee shop/grocery store/art gallery, our answering machine didn't pick up. There was still no power further south. We camped that night deep in the forest just a stone's throw from the road and cooked hot dogs and drank beer that we chilled in a creek. It had been just about the best bike day we had ever shared.

The next morning we woke in the quiet of the woods, but as the sun climbed overhead, more cars began to share the swerving road with lumber trucks. And instead of tooting horns there were honks and the screeches of braking wheels, and we were shunted further to the side of the road. The riding had been so good that we had become spoiled, so the few close calls that we had with trucks, which neither shared the road nor slowed as they sped past, were unnerving. Riding single file now, we were still more than a few times a bit late to jerk our bikes off the pavement and into the gravel swale as an overloaded logging truck screamed past. Conversation was replaced with barked, "Car back!" We held our breath during air horn blasts and hoped the passing passenger doors of the Ford F-650s and Chevy King Cabs were unadorned with outrigger-size rearview mirrors.

There was still an hour of daylight, so we coasted into a cluster of buildings that consisted of one motel, one roadhouse, and one general store. We had made it to a place called Meyer's Flat, and we were both relieved to call it a day. Both of us were looking forward to a hot shower, a hot dinner, and cold beer. We leaned our bikes up against a massive tree, which loomed over the motel's flat roof, and walked next door to the general store. The general store, the motel, and the road-house all shared the same owners, management, and employees, who were now seated in a semicircle on folding chairs on the wooden storefront of the general store. Their attention was fixed on a huge TV that spanned the length of three milk crates. Bowls of chips and salsa, potato chips, and bottles of beer littered their boots.

Marc opened with, "Hi."

Only two of the five faces looked up from the TV, and only one didn't seem put out. The nicest face in the group, a woman's whose graying hair was bunched into a ponytail, finally spoke, "We're closed."

The cord from the TV snaked across the planks of the storefront, past the old wooden doors propped open by two statues of Bigfoot.

All the lights in the store were on. And there was one guy inside bending over into the open glass door of the beer cooler wrestling to get a six-pack off the top shelf without tearing its cardboard box.

"Closed?" Marc repeated.

The upturned face that hadn't smiled said, "Closed. Yeah." Then we looked around at the other figures in the semicircle that nodded and scuffled their boots in affirmation. One of them piped up, "For the game," and drank from his bottle until it was upside down and empty in his upturned mouth.

"What game?" I asked.

Marc nudged me, but too late. Now all the faces looked up at us. Marc tried to hide behind me. He removed his sweaty baseball cap and ran his fingers over his hair and his chin whiskers and hissed at me, "The Super Bowl." Marc then lowered his cap to his lap, trying to cover his Lycra-clad package with it.

Parked bumper to bumper in the dirt along the edge of the road across the street were a half dozen Ford F-750s with the occasional Chevy King Cab just to be different.

"We just want to get a room and a bite to eat," I smiled.

I knew my best chance was to try to maintain eye contact with the woman who had first looked up. "The diner is closed," she said with some finality as she rose from her chair and turned away from me, walking through the open doors of the general store. From over her shoulder she added, "But I'll check you in. Each room's got a microwave."

I took a step to follow her into the store, afraid that if I hesitated, she might change her mind. Marc wavered a bit. I knew he didn't want to be left all alone in front of those other guys, naked as he was in his black spandex shorts, powder blue ankle socks, and pink polka-dot, form-fitting top. But I knew he also didn't want to walk past those guys either, as I was about to, to enter the store.

"Honey," I said, deciding to save his ass, "why don't you unload all those heavy bags from our bikes and check to see if your chain needs lube, while I check us in and pick up a few things for supper?"

Marc thought things through for a second. "Hey baby," he decided, "why don't you check us in and pick up a few things for dinner?" And then in a louder voice which carried past the seated men and into the store, "I'm gonna unload our bags and work on our equipment. Might wanna check some a those welds." Then he turned back toward the motel and crabbed off sort of sideways, so none of the guys could see his butt.

I swooped down the store's three aisles and filled my crooked arm with a can of turkey chili, a bag of tortilla chips, a jar of salsa, and from the beer cooler two big bottles of Sierra Nevada. The man who had been wrestling to pull out a six-pack graciously stood aside for me, checking out my butt while I bent over to reach in.

Back at the counter as the woman was ringing me up, she asked, "Where you going to on them bicycles?"

"Eureka, I guess."

"Well then, you got quite a ways."

"Yes but, it's fun."

"Fun, huh. Just be careful all the same. This road's pretty dangerous. Lots a tourists lookin' 'round the whole time not payin' attention. And deer jumping out of the woods all the time causing accidents." The woman handed me back my card and the slip to sign.

"Thanks. We're always careful."

The man's voice joined in from behind me. "Up the road a bit we had one just go down not long ago."

"Sure did," the woman nodded at first and then shook her head, "Franky ruined that truck a his."

"Sure did," the man agreed.

It was quiet while the woman was bagging our dinner, so I felt like I should say something. "That's a shame. Was he injured?"

"Nah, nah. He's okay. Just a pretty good scare, that's all. And some missed work," the man said.

I smiled to show that I was relieved that Franky wasn't hurt.

Still facing me, the woman stood up on her toes reaching overhead to a shelf that ran the length of the register counter. From behind the impulse items, she pulled down a heavy brass key, which was embossed with the numeral 4, and handed it to me.

"Bike rider's dead, though," she added.

"Sure is," the man agreed.

"What bike rider?" I asked. Now it was their turn to look surprised.

"Why, the one I was just tellin' you 'bout," the woman said.

I still didn't get it. "You were talking about how Franky damaged his truck when he hit a deer."

"No. It was a bike rider that got hit," the man said as he plunked his six-pack on the counter beside my bag.

I was flustered. I reached for my bag and stepped back. Looking at them both I said, "You shouldn't speak that way. You shouldn't say, 'One just went down,' like that. Like you're talking about a downed cow. That's a person. People don't go down! People get killed!"

I could see by their faces that I wasn't making myself understood. They weren't getting it, and I was getting agitated. "You shouldn't say stuff like, 'A bike rider got hit.' He didn't 'get hit.' That Franky guy hit him. Franky killed him—with his truck. Franky killed that bike rider with his truck."

We left early in the morning to beat the traffic out of Meyer's Flat.

Riding a bike on the road can be dangerous. Even when you couldn't imagine a better place—the redwood coast of California—or a better time to be riding your bike, like during a regional power outage. Or along the same hilly wooded lane with my brother that we used to coast down as little kids. If there are cars on that road, it can be like swimming in a tank full of sharks.

Okay. So, what to do about it? How to cope with cars?

To begin with, know your rights, know the rules, and know the road. It's not that bad, really, and there are a couple of coping mechanisms that you can use to reach an honorable peace with yourself.

Know Your Rights

Without being too legalistic, when you're riding your bike on the road, you should arm yourself with the confidence that you have a legal right to the road. I know it's difficult to imagine that bicycles have just as much a legal right to the road as do cars, but it's true nonetheless. Notwithstanding the ubiquitous second-class status imposed on us by traffic planners, police, and car drivers, cyclists and pedestrians have even more license to the roads than do cars. And who says? The US Constitution.

The constitution limits the right of the government to restrict the rights of the citizens. That's really all it is. It says right in there that our rights are "inalienable and endowed by the creator." Part of our rights as citizens are the cyclists' rights to the road.

But there is a common misconception that because the Constitution and the Bill of Rights do not spell out the right to ride your bike, riding your bike must, therefore, be a privilege. And that privilege to ride your bike is kind of a pain for society at large, and so we should be happy and grateful to be shunted off to the broken glass—strewn gutter at the far side of the road. After all, they are being nice to us. They don't have to let us ride our bikes at all!

The word *bicycle* cannot be found in the Constitution, because bicycles had not yet been invented. And so, similarly, the right to ride a bike on the road is clearly spelled out elsewhere in that document and can be found in the phrase "freedom of movement." Just substitute the word *horse* or *horse and buggy* for the word *bicycle* and you can easily see that the framers intended very few limitations on the right of the people to travel for work or pleasure on public roads. At the time that the Constitution defined the government's authority and power to limit travel on public roads, the vast majority of travel on those roads was by foot. And so pedestrians, horse riders, and hay wagons have "the most" right to the public roads.

The whole body of traffic laws, The Vehicle Code, is grounded on the precept that the government's authority to limit our right to drive requires that in the interest of public safety, drivers must stop at red lights, turn the wheels to the curb when parked on a hill, and remain 200 feet behind fire engines. If we drivers don't do those things, then we lose our license to drive. That is a pretty big reason to pay attention to all the traffic laws when driving a car: the loss of your driver's license.

When they first started to appear on the streets, bicycles were indeed required to be licensed in some big cities. Back then, they were a menace to the horse and buggy crowd and to the pedestrians. There weren't too many big cities, so the movement to require bike licenses only took hold in a few of the oldest and largest cities, mainly on the East Coast and in the Midwest. Within a few short years, the squawking to regulate bicycles was drowned out by the clamor to regulate cars. And as America and the auto have grown up together over the last 100 years, bicycles have been forgotten.

But most places where we live now, like suburbs, were not cities then. In these suburbs, there are no old and long-forgotten statutes on the books that regulate cyclists. And though I'm not a lawyer, I don't believe that there is a single state that requires a cyclist to be licensed. There are certainly sections of the vehicle code that do pertain to bikes, and they do have to be followed unless you want to get a ticket.

The absence of a requirement by the state to obtain a cycling license means that cycling is one of those pesky inalienable rights, and not just a privilege. As a cyclist, you do have a right to the road, the whole road if you wish, as long as you don't violate any other sections of the vehicle code. If you ride cognizant of your rights to the road, I'm sure that you not only will be safer on the road, but also will enjoy your ride a whole lot more.

Know the Rules

Okay. We have a right to the road. So what?

The roads might still be polluted with bullies, especially in certain parts of this country. Not much you can do about that, except make yourself feel better by occasionally blowing them a kiss. But as a cyclist, if you know and follow the rules and insist that the bullies follow them as well, your road riding experiences might be more pleasurable than my hellish freshman-year memories.

The first rule of the road is really an unwritten one. And that all-important primary rule is: Better to be wronged and alive, than right and lying in a ditch. I'm sure you already know that rule and its various other versions such as, "An SUV will always win" and "Might makes right."

You may know that the traffic code says that as a cyclist you have a right to take the whole lane, but if that soccer mom in the Volvo wagon behind you is really serious about not being late for the big game, then pull off to the side and let her pass you. If you have a feeling that an overtaking car is passing you at warp speed only to yank a right-hand turn right in front of you in order to drop off their video, rely on your gut instead of your reasoning that the driver would never behave that way if you were in a car and not on your road bike.

But if you ride and obey the laws, the cars on the road will probably respect your rights. Cars are more likely to treat you as a car if you behave in traffic like a car.

Dealing with traffic

David Smith

For the most part, when in traffic, ride cautiously, as though you are just another car, maybe a cute Mini Cooper, and you'll be just fine. Politely use hand signals and give a wave of thanks. Courtesy really works. But if you want to clear up any roadside confusion you might encounter, you might do as my boyfriend Marc has done for years. In his beat-up messenger bag he carries a small laminated card printed on both sides in very tiny but legible type with the Top 10 rules of the vehicle code . . . like the section that says that bikes should make left-hand turns from the left-hand lane. And a popular one, that bikes do not have to pull over while on a grade until there are five cars behind them in traffic.

Putting on the left turn signals

David Smith

RULES OF THE ROAD

This is a summary of the bicycle section of the California Vehicle Code. Readers are advised to check the vehicle code in their state for more detailed information and actual wording.

21200.5. It is against the law to ride a bicycle while under the influence of alcohol or drugs.

21201. Bicycles must be equipped with a brake that is able to make one braked wheel skid on dry, level, clean pavement.

Handlebars must not be higher than the rider's shoulders.

The bicycle must be small enough for the rider to stop safely, support it upright with a foot on the ground, and restart safely.

Every bicycle ridden at night must have the following equipment.

• White headlight, or a white light attached to the rider and visible from a distance of 300 feet in front and from the sides of the bicycle

• A red rear reflector, visible to 500 feet when illuminated by a motor vehicle's headlights

• A white or yellow reflector on each pedal visible from the front and rear of the bicycle from a distance of 200 feet

• A white or yellow side reflector on each side of the front portion of the bicycle and a white or red reflector on each side of the rear portion of the bicycle—or—reflectorized tires

21202. Bicyclists traveling slower than the normal speed of traffic shall ride as close as practicable to the right-hand edge of the roadway except under any of the following situations.

• When overtaking and passing another bicycle or vehicle

• When preparing for a left turn

• To avoid hazards that make it unsafe to stay to the far right, including lanes too narrow to share side by side with another vehicle

• When approaching a right turn

21203. Bicyclists may not attach their bicycle or themselves to another vehicle in motion.

21204. The bicycle must have a permanent and regular seat.

Passengers must have a separate seat, and passengers 4 years old or younger, or weighing 40 pounds or less, must be restrained, protected from the moving parts of the bicycle, and wear a helmet meeting ASTM or Snell standards.

21205. Bicyclists may not carry any package, bundle, or article which prevents the operator from keeping at least one hand upon the handlebars.

21206. This chapter does not prevent local authorities, by ordinance, from regulating the registration of bicycles and the parking and operation of bicycles on pedestrian or bicycle facilities, be provided such regulation is not in conflict with the provisions of this code. Check with your local jurisdictions for information about such ordinances.

21208. Bicyclists traveling slower than normal traffic must ride in established bike lanes except to pass another bicycle or vehicle, when preparing to make a left or right turn, or to avoid debris or hazardous conditions.

21209. No person shall drive a motor vehicle in a bicycle lane established on a roadway, except as follows:

• To park where parking is permitted

• To enter or leave the roadway

• To prepare for a turn within a distance of 200 feet from the intersection

This section does not prohibit the use of a motorized bicycle in a bicycle lane, at a speed no greater than is reasonable or prudent, having due regard for visibility, traffic conditions, and the condition of the roadway surface of the bicycle lane, and in a manner which does not endanger the safety of bicyclists.

21210. It is illegal to leave a bicycle on its side on a sidewalk, or to park it in any way that blocks pedestrians.

21211. No person shall stop, stand, sit, loiter, or park a bicycle or vehicle upon any public or private bike path or trail, if their actions block the normal and reasonable movement of any bicyclist.

21212. Bicyclists and bicycle passengers under 18 years of age must wear a properly fitted and fastened bicycle helmet that meets ASTM or Snell standards.

21650.1. Bicyclists on the shoulder of a roadway must ride in the same direction as traffic on the roadway.

21960. Bicyclists may not ride on freeways where signs prohibit it.

23330. Bicyclists may not cross a toll bridge unless permitted by signs.

27400. Bicyclists may not wear earplugs in both ears or a headset covering both ears. This section does not apply to hearing aids.

If a motorist wishes to pull over and tell you what he thinks of your riding regarding the rules of the road, whipping out your lammy and quoting from it does the world a better turn than quoting Dick Cheney. You have the right to take a whole lane as you ride in order to ensure your own safety if the right side of the road is littered with broken glass, or if you think a car door might open up suddenly.

Marc also ascribes to the section of the code that mandates a horn audible up to 100 feet. Hose-clamped next to his thumb shifter is a small marine air horn primarily used on boats. And he uses it in traffic when he feels the need. That makes him feel important.

If you live in an area with enough population density to support a Starbucks, then you may also discover that 4:45 P.M. is not the best time to ride.

Know the Road

Know the rush hour. The inherent danger posed by poor civic planning, road rage, and the cyclist's lowly status on the roads can make riding during the early morning and late afternoon challenging.

Dave and I were only out a few weeks into our Century training rides before I saw a side of my brother I had forgotten existed. Sure, when we were kids, my brothers used to chase each other with sticks and scream, "BLAM! You're dead!" I thought then that my brothers' cruelty knew no bounds. They heaved rocks at squirrels and would have launched boulders at deer had they the projectile strength in their skinny arms. The berber carpet in the television room was a wrestling mat on which were settled such momentous issues as who ate the last fudge pop or who was going to volunteer to rake up the leaves in the yard. But 20 or 30 years later, you forget those *Lord of the Flies* afternoons, so when a passing car zoomed in on Dave and me and blasted its horn for good measure, my jaw slackened as Dave took off after it.

There was no way he was going to catch that speeding Ford Bronco, but Dave lunged like a frothing junkyard dog after the Bronco's diminishing trailer hitch. And after about 50 feet of furious sprinting and foul language, Dave was yanked to a panting stop like a junkyard dog with its chain snapping tight against its throat. He slunk through the perimeter of a large retreating circle while I caught up.

"Feel better?"

"I just hate when they do that! I mean, come on. There's nobody out here!" Dave waved dismissively with his hand to the muddy green fields that stretched beyond us. The road was narrow and winding and without traffic lights or even stop signs. Clusters of brightly painted mailboxes perched on pressure-treated posts every quarter of a mile or so, some shaped like ornate tiny doll's houses, and more than a few were Home Depot thin metal Quonset huts. These mailboxes were further proof that the irregularly spaced boxy shapes that dotted those greening fields weren't bales of stacked hay. They were brick-faced, great-roomed Colonials and particle board–turreted Victorians, and new age Amish farmhouses.

We really should have been upset with ourselves. That's really what road rage is, simply the expression of exasperation that we all feel from putting ourselves in a jam. Dave and I had been riding side by side, just gabbing away about what an awesome day it was, how lucky Dave had been to sneak away from his computer, and how jealous John would be when Dave told him how great his new bike felt. Neither of us had heard the squeal and heavy drone of the Bronco as it reined itself in behind us, curve after country road curve.

It's the same when I'm riding by myself, just jamming with Eric Clapton on my iPod, ignoring the cars behind me that want to pass. Their resentment builds and then explodes in a roaring cloud of exhaust fumes. Since there are going to be cars on the road with me, I cover one ear with the headphones' speaker. The other speaker I set behind my ear. That way I can still keep an ear out for the sounds of approaching cars. And mono Jerry is still way better than no Jerry at all.

I let Dave half wheel me while he calmed himself down. A few miles down the road, the shoulder widened, and I pulled alongside. "Don't let it bother you."

"Okay, okay. I'm not. But you see what I mean. Why does he have to honk just as he's passing us, not way back down the road when we can do something about it, like single up or move over or something?"

"Dave, just enjoy the ride and understand that that guy is probably already at home feeling uptight every day whether he honks at a cyclist or not. You're riding your bike because it makes you feel good. So let it."

For the next half hour, as we rode in single file, I let him get on my wheel and increased the pace. The cleansing feeling of speed would make him feel better. In fact, we both quickly forgot all about that Bronco.

While out on the road, even if you're doing the right thing by following the rules of the road, you have to always remember why you're out there. And that's to feel good.

Dave's Training Log— Week 6

Date	Sleep/Wt.	Workout	Notes
Mon	6 hrs/168		
Tue	7 hrs/168	1.5 hrs	Felt good on favorite loop; hit hills pretty hard; good warmup
Wed	8 hrs/169		(No time)
Thu	8 hrs/168		
Fri	7 hrs/167		(Still no time to even look at bike)
Sat	7 hrs/167	Situps and pushups with kids	
Sun	8 hrs/168	1.5 hrs	FINALLY got to get out! Moderate pace, 21 miles on a new route; car almost ran us off the road

Total Riding Hours: **3**
Total Miles: **45**

Marla's Training Log— Week 6

Date	Sleep/HR/Wt.	Workout	Notes
Mon	9 hrs/42/140	30 min run zones 2–3	Felt fine
		1.5 hrs: zone 2	During spin, crashed on descent while racing a car; hurt right shoulder, neck, hand
Tue	9 hrs/46/141	1 hr at zones 1–2	Easy to gym—sore!
		30 min at gym: core workout	(Worked on bike for 2 hrs)
Wed	9 hrs/45/141	2 hrs: zones 3–4	Great solo road ride, although hand is still sore; hit hills hard; chain keeps slipping
Thu	9 hrs/48/141	2 hrs: zones 1–3	Another photo shoot—lots of slow riding up the hill, then quick bursts for shots; felt good
Fri	8 hrs/46/140	2 hrs: zones 2–3	Ride with group from local shop—moderate pace; felt decent, but sat in often
Sat	9 hrs/49/140	1.5 hr spin: zone 2	Lovely ride on coast; motocross—easy ride to get used to handlebar; good upper body workout
Sun	7 hrs/46/139	5 hrs: zones 2–4	Much longer ride than planned but held on okay; ready for a whole day off!

Total Hours: **16**

DAY 43 THROUGH 49 . . .
THE EQUIPMENT

CHAPTER
7

"Most of us wouldn't be roadies at all if we weren't bike geeks first."

—*an unknown bike geek*

A perfectly good bike leaned against the drywall in Dave's tidy garage. A really nice bike in fact. But we made a deal, anyway. If we both were able to stick with this training plan for a Century Ride, then I'd see what I could do to help out with a new bike for him. "Down the road," I cautioned.

If after a couple of weeks of riding your old bike or your friend's, you truly believe that a new bike won't be relegated to the basement along with the moldy weight lifting bench, then by all means indulge yourself. Help out the bike industry. A new bike can be an excellent motivator for your Century training plan as well. It's a big, fat, juicy carrot, or carrot cake if you prefer, that is well earned for your hard riding. But though it can be a nice thing, a fancy shmancy new bike isn't always necessary.

Dave and I kept our cadence side by side during the afternoons. Me on my tricked-out, finger-light, black roadster. And he on his minutely scratched, top-tube-decal, guilty-of-ghost-shifting, old bike. The unspoken protocol about trying out another's bike prevented Dave from actually asking me. You can borrow a buddy's bike, but Emily Seatpost's as yet unwritten *Guide to Roadie Etiquette* advises that you refrain from actually swinging a leg over the top tube and squirming into the saddle right in front of your obliging friend. Once while I was stuffing my ponytail into my helmet before our ride, I admit that I allowed Dave a few furtive finger pulls of my velvety front brake. I then wiped the oily imprint he left on my lever with the palm of my glove. Bike lust exists, no doubt. It was easy to catch Dave's green-eyed glances reflecting from the gleam of my double-butted double diamond. I'd put a half wheel between us.

As we rode and then basked in the warmth of our exertion, we chatted and I teased about the possibility of a new bike for him. "We'll see," I'd say to cap the conversation.

During our rides, he was a strong negotiator for bike swag. And an aggressive gambler. At the start of one of our innumerable town sign sprints, a chocolate mare and her shiny colt just a few feet away on the other side of the white fence momentarily distracted me. Dave took advantage of this rare girlie moment and took off. The sign leaned at the crest of a small hill less than 100 feet up the cracked asphalt.

Dave yelled over his shoulder, "Winner's choice!" His challenge caused the colt to skitter away from the fence. The aroma of sweet grass and horse was too thick for me to get on top of my gear. With a flick of my wrist, I could have clicked into a bigger gear. But I didn't. Dave spun past the road sign of an animal's silhouette in a circle with a slash across it. I gained but couldn't catch on to Dave's back, hunched as much as the signpost was bent, as though each were out of breath having just made it to the top of the hill. At the top, I rolled past the imaginary town border, greeting the face of defeat. And Dave's face beamed, "I want a new bike!"

I hate to lose. Even as a kid, I never let my little brother, Chris, beat me at pool or when shooting free throws. I am 6 years older than Chris, so by the time he reached the age that he could pin me at arm wrestling, I was off to college and no longer interested in sibling competitions. Or so I thought.

The sprinting stakes between Dave and me up to this point had topped out at a post-ride juice smoothie, occasionally upping it double or nothing to a pale ale, either of which I always enjoyed to the last drop. Dave's wheeling and dealing for new parts for his old bike never surpassed some fresh bar tape.

When I was a kid, the hand-me-downs from my older brothers John, Dave, and Mark were my true treasures. The blown-out tennis racket was a prized possession. The scuffed and dinged deck of the skateboard was so revered, I never dared to even replace my brothers' faded and unrecognizable stickers with my own. Mark was closest to me in age. In our backyard Dave always struggled to run in the footsteps of John, the oldest. Rather than chase after Dave, for some reason Mark usually chose to go slow so I could catch up. Mark lobbed me the easy volleys that I could return over the hedges whose height my buckteeth barely reached. He was the one who carved curves down the driveway with me gamely skating his line. Dave played it cool by fingering the fuzz on his upper lip, while John mysteriously chose instead to sit cross-legged on the lawn and talk softly with the girls with Farrah Fawcett hair from down the road. I'd run up to the top of the driveway holding my skateboard above my sweaty bangs in triumph, beaming because Mark let me catch up, smiling.

Dave and I let the small hill carry us down the road, and we were kids again. This time closer in age. This time, it was Dave who was victorious, and I, magnanimous, as Mark had been. "Okay. Okay. I'll make a few calls and see what I can do," I smiled. That never happens when I lose. Somehow, even though Mark had been gone for many years now, I felt closer to him, too.

Dave's grin stretched from ear to ear like the chin strap of his helmet, and he pumped his hands overhead in the air. "Just like yours!" he yelled with hoarse specificity.

It felt really rewarding to let Dave wrangle from me one of the last few Santa Cruz road frames left in their warehouse. Even a pro has to cash in a lot of chips to score a new bike. I had erroneously thought I could entice Dave to help me out with this Century project for maybe a Timbuk2 messenger bag. An old set of wheels at the most.

I didn't feel too bad hitting up Rob Roskopp, owner of Santa Cruz Bicycles, after he admitted they were completely discontinuing their road frames because they were so swamped trying to fill orders for their mountain bikes. Still, before we hung up, I ended up promising Rob that there would be full-page thick paper glossy photos of his donated frame. I hope I can swing that.

With good reason, most people buy their bikes already built up from a bike store. The economy, compatibility, warranty, and goodwill of the bike shop makes the decision to buy an already built-up bike a no-brainer 99 percent of the time.

Bikes are funny things because, unlike televisions, cars, or most other consumer goods, there is no manufacturer that sells a bike that's completely designed and fabricated in-house. From the earliest days, a complete bike has been made from the ingenuity of a number of different designers, whose components may or may not fit well with each other. You'd think someone by now would have come up with the great idea to design and manufacture a bicycle as a complete unit from the drawing board all the way through the various forms of production and deliver it at the retail level to the bike store, and then into the sweaty palms of an excited new owner. But as far as I know, only one crazy genius, Alex Pong, who was working for Cannondale at the time, has done so. And I'm pretty sure he quit after one bike. Like the video game with the same name, where the Pong bicycle is I have no idea, but I'm sure someone at Cannondale made sure to protect it as an asset during their Chapter 13 reorganization.

A few manufacturers of bike frames are huge multinational corporations with extensive research and development operations, which are able to deliver incredible value for supremely engineered and fastidiously fabricated frames from exotic materials like carbon fiber, titanium, manganese, aluminum, and composites of all. These large, reputable builders—American, European, and Asian—all stand behind their products with various warranties and customer service agreements. Some have been in the business for more than a century.

There are also dozens of boutique builders as well, whose attention to detail and knowledge of material science and access to precision machine tooling have expanded the range of frames that they can supply to even the recreational rider. These boutique builders are the quintessential small business owner. Often, employees have some ownership stake, and it shows in their workmanship. Typically the founder, once an active racer, may still be a hands-on CEO. Frames from builders like these are revered by bike geeks for their near mythic qualities. Some examples are Swift, Ibis, and Alan.

A work of art might cost some money, but my boyfriend Marc, who apprenticed for years with a custom builder whose shop was more stunning than some of the art galleries in Sausalito, swears that custom frames are often traded for computer work, medical care, or a new roof.

Although most reasonably healthy people can ride almost any kind of bike and easily complete Century Rides, I recommend sticking with the traditional double-diamond, skinny tire—type bike. Leave the mountain bikes to the dirt, the fat-tire cruisers for the beach, the unicycles for the circus. Recumbents can actually be more aerodynamically efficient than traditional bikes under certain conditions. However, recumbents are unable to benefit from the even more aerodynamic efficiencies of riding in a peloton and are tough on steep climbs. True, you might be really fast on a recumbent, but you'd probably be riding much of the Century alone.

If we owned a tandem, maybe I could get my boyfriend Marc to do more than the start of a Century Ride. Moms and dads smiling the whole way have pulled trailers with the kids in tow.

The manufacturers of the bike components like stems, saddles, wheels, and even water bottle cages all mirror these three levels of scale: the lone artisan, the boutique builder, and the large corporation. Most roadies go for Shimano or Campagnolo groupos. Of course, Shimano would be my number one recommendation. Their design, reliability, and value are unmatched by any other company.

The most important element of any bike that you choose to train on is the fit. And although books have been written on the subject, regardless of gigabytes of computer modeling, the fit of a bicycle is a subjective art. So imagine how difficult it would be to select a frame size and its geometry. Then pick and choose its components: stem length and rise, bar width, saddle height and position on its rails, and crank arm length. And then imagine how much more difficult it would be to assemble it all together and have the fit work out perfectly.

The fit of a rider new to the sport might include a tall stem and straight bar with a rise and slight curve at the ends. After some time on the road, as you strengthen the core muscles of your trunk, you'll find that you want to ride with a flatter back. You'll feel more com-

Santa Cruz's aluminum rig

fortable with a lower position; you'll want to stretch the rider's cockpit by sliding the saddle all the way back and reaching out with a longer stem. As you become more fit, you might want to adjust your bike fit.

Even a serious cyclist sometimes starts the season with a softer saddle. The fit for an elite roadie can even change depending on the expected course conditions: a seat post raised a millimeter or two for a hill climb, perhaps a wider bar in anticipation of a lot of sprints and attacks. Lance Armstrong is know for tinkering, in nanoincrements, and testing new hand positions and elbow angles.

For a new rider, the fit of the saddle itself is a big issue. Don't be intimidated by it. In the bike magazines, the photos of saddles make them appear as narrow and sharp as stilettos. In the bike shop, the seats on the demo bike that seem to fit might resemble a small waterbed with sheepskin sheets. Those are only good for coffee shop rides. Choose the saddle that has good support for your sit bones, is relatively narrow, and is pliant where it really counts. Fizik and Selle

Shimano drivetrain

Italia are very popular brands and are Italian made, which is good. You might want to ask the bike shop guy or gal what they recommend for you.

A secret from the pro peloton is that no matter what saddle a rider starts the season with, if the time off the saddle has been longer than a few weeks, there is a good chance there will be a wince of butt pain. The size and shape of the saddle really doesn't have as much to do with your saddle sores as the time in the saddle. It won't make a difference if you're sitting on a saddle of the whitest fleece, on the thickest gel whose precise contours were taken from the depression in the Aeron chair in your office: Your butt will still hurt. You still have to get used to your saddle.

If you continue to put the time on your bike, the discomfort will diminish over the next few rides. The nerves scream for you to stop, but they quiet down after they realize you aren't paying any attention. You'll be surprised when you reach the conclusion that a smaller saddle might actually fit better. By the time you're ready for your

Your saddle is a very personal choice.

Century Ride, the saddle that fits you best will be a close approximation of those scary leather stilettos that gave you the shivers in the bike magazines. In general, the least amount of saddle surface in contact with your naughty bits, the smaller the chances are for saddle sores. The newest saddle designs feature strategically placed holes. A few companies—Terry Precision Saddles comes to mind first—design saddles with female anatomy as the main criterion. I know there's a Specialized saddle designed for the male anatomy.

Women, and those guys with some preexisting medical conditions, will have some specific concerns about saddles that I'll address in the Pain Hurts in a Good Way chapter on page 153. At this point, only a few weeks into the training plan, it is highly unlikely that the riding to date might aggravate a medical condition. If you have any second thoughts or concerns, consult a physician.

The short list of items to keep in mind about the fit of your bike while out on the road during the first few weeks is just that, a short list. The really serious cyclist probably has already built up a reference library of technical manuals; leaning, yellowed stacks of *VeloNews;* bound volumes of *Bicycling* magazine; and milk crates of various parts catalogs. If you're thinking about upgrading to a new bike or buying your first since puberty, when you're ready to seriously start shopping, make sure you walk right past the big box store.

The big box stores like Wal-Mart or Price Club do sell bikes. They sell bikes at prices that can't be beat, but you'd lose if you bought your Century bike there. It is very doubtful that any of their employees would be able to help you with the short list of items you need to keep in mind while looking for a bike that fits. Whereas any decent independent bike dealer will proudly walk you right over to their Serotta Size Cycle fitting tool kit.

The Serotta fitting tool is a universally adjustable stationary bike. A certified shop employee can accommodate a range of body types from Shaquille O'Neal to Danny DeVito on this frame fitter. And if you happen to forget the short list below, the shop employee usually has a very long checklist to work from.

- Stand-over height

- Saddle type, tilt, height, and fore-and-aft position

- Bar length and sweep, drop, and curve

- Stem height, length, and negative or positive rise

- Crank arm length and spindle width

- The geometry of the frame itself in relation to your body and riding style

So, even though Dave and I built up his bike, I strongly recommend that most people rely on the expertise and artistry of an independent bicycle dealer in order to get the fit just right. Sometimes, if your local bike shop doesn't use the Serotta system, the shop can still fit you with the experienced eye of the shop's bike shop guy or gal. You can feel comfortable being fitted in the hands of such a person if his hands are thickly calloused. The fingertips from the third knuckle past the second knuckle should be darkly tanned, and yet below the first knuckle all the way to the wrist, the skin should be smooth and starkly white. If the helper is wearing a slightly too tight wool jersey in garish colors with Euro scribbling all over it, you'll probably be fine.

A good bike shop will ask you what kind of riding you expect to be doing: Don't be bashful. Tell the person helping you that you're planning on your first Century Ride. The shop might have a better idea of the reality of your Century Ride experience than you imagine. Most people, elites and novices, either assume that they'll be in the lead group to cross the line or that they might drop out. Both usually find out that neither is the case.

If you have been studiously reading this book, skimming the relevant magazines, Web surfing, and generally fantasizing, then you should be able to ask the shop employees all the questions that you'll have about other equipment.

Regardless of your level of cycling ability at some point during your life, you'll have to answer as honestly as you can the following question, "Lycra or baggy?" Don't let any of the models in the magazines influence your decision . . . they all look good.

True, no one in the Tour de France wears baggy shorts. And maybe you don't either. But I recommend that you ask this question of yourself before a close friend asks you in a roundabout way if you should revisit the issue.

The classic chamois shorts, formfitting, typically black, between midthigh and the top of the knee in length, are padded with a high-tech diaper that wicks away sweat and makes for an overall more hygienically healthy and comfortable ride. The back of the short is cut higher to prevent plumber's butt as you hunch over. The tight fit eliminates chafe the same way the leather saddle does, by reducing the incidences of surface friction. The formfitting chamois also reduces the wind resistance as you pedal and is unlikely to get snagged on the horn of your saddle or on an errant bar end. Castelli, Pearl Izumi, and Sugoi all make excellent spandex shorts.

A word of caution: Do not attempt to spray a pair of chamois with any water repellent. Let them get wet; you can always shower later. Chamois usually are stinky enough without actually trying to trap inside them every drop of your body's moisture.

The baggy short, a relatively recent innovation that has crossed over from the free-riding mountain bikers, has advantages, too. Basically, baggy shorts are a pair of chamoised spandex hiding under some Bermuda shorts. Baggies may have pockets and a more civilized look in the ATM line, but they are not as aero, tend to bunch up, and don't breathe as well on hot rides.

Oakley, Sugoi, and Nema are some of the top brands that most bike shops carry. They are all well made, functional, and stylish, and will protect your assets a little better if you take a spill.

The thing is, the choice of which type of short to ride in is a personal one. When you're inside the changing room at the bike shop, make sure the door is locked and then look in the mirror. The classier shops usually have a bench along one of the cubicle's walls on which you can sit down to collect yourself for a moment if you don't like what you see.

I wear spandex, but not all the time. If I plan to ride through one of Baltimore's sketchier neighborhoods, I wear baggies. I feel like I look more like a boy that way. Less likely to be hassled. Similarly, when a good friend of mine was living in San Diego, he prided himself on never wearing the "uncool" baggy shorts. That is, until the evening he was riding his skinny road bike along the beachfront boardwalk, his blonde mullet tucked into a smart ponytail that trailed midway down the back of his neon tank top, and his tight-chamois-wearing butt got slapped by a surfer dude as he rolled past. My buddy still wears spandex, but when he rides along the boardwalk, he wears baggies.

The helmet, the eyewear, and even half-fingered riding gloves are not optional equipment. You want to be wearing them on every ride. Helmets have come a long way since the thickly padded leather straps of the Euro brain bucket. Modern helmets are light, well-ventilated, and effective, three things the traditional helmets of pelotons in years past lacked. Watch the Tour de France on TV, envy them, and be inspired by them. Don't let your eyes linger on the unprotected noggins of some of the Tour's leaders. Pro cyclists can be knuckleheads; take it from one who knows.

Whether you choose to buy a new Giro or an alien-looking Rudy Project helmet, make sure it's ASTM or Snell approved. At some of the best bike shops, it occasionally happens that a customer walks out with a skateboarding or motocross helmet after a miscommunication with a shop employee.

Your eyewear also is not a joking matter. Your shades protect your eyes whether it's sunny, dry, windy, or rainy. Also, your choice of sunglasses will dictate how many friends you make on the ride. Although quality polarized eyewear is expensive, you might as well spend a little more on eyewear with easily replaceable lenses. I've worn Oakleys for 11 years as a pro rider. I think their optics are the best and, of course, they look the coolest.

Regardless of what kind of helmet you wear, make sure you tuck the frames of your eyewear *over* the straps of your helmet. It's a safety issue. With the eyewear frames tucked over the straps, you're less

I don't leave home without my Giro and Oakleys.

likely to be hit with the empty water bottle of a buddy who possesses a greater sense of style. Some consider it uncool to wear the straps over your eyewear.

Similarly, on every ride I wear gloves. Not only do the gloves afford some relief from the vibration that a really stiff bike setup can shimmy from every pebble on the road all the way to your cramping palms, if you should spill on a patch of gravel, you would much rather pick gravel out of your gloved palm than out of your ungloved lifeline. The back of the glove is also a great place to wipe the snot from your nose if done with style. Depending on the weather, you want to think about full- or half-finger gloves, insulated or waterproofed. Your dad's golf gloves or your kid's baseball batting gloves can work, but the cycling-specific gloves make more sense.

The options for shoes are limited by their very functionality. All the cycling shoes sort of look the same. I've worn Shimano for years and have had great success with them. Sidi makes excellent shoes, and many pros swear by them. All of these shoes perform nicely with the major pedal systems: Shimano, Time, and Speedplay. You want to avoid the old-style strap-on toe clip. Even though the simplicity of toe clips may be initially very appealing, the inherent inefficiencies in energy transfer will drive you crazy on a serious ride. You should invest in a pedal system and shoes at the same time you're throwing down for a new bike. Occasionally, a minute change in the pedal platform's height can wreak havoc on your perfect fit. The bike shop will help you with tuning the pedal and adjusting your sole's attachment point. A cool consideration to keep in mind when shopping for shoes is a recess in the sole so that you can walk around easier and quieter. These casual bike shoes may not be as light or stiff as the dedicated racing shoe, but they're a great compromise for anybody who plans on pushing their bike for a few miles.

And as long as you have opened your wallet, if you have the means and desire, you might want to splurge on a few other items that are probably displayed in a locked case. Cycle computers, heart rate monitors, power meters, and iPods are really nice, but none are necessary. Later on in the training plan as the mileage builds, I'll explain why you may want to consider their utility.

After Dave had put in a few rides on his new bike, we realized he needed a longer stem. He was a little taller than I had remembered. He wanted to pick up a few other small things; he had lost a minipump during one of our screaming descents the week before, and he needed some patches. And other stuff. So we rolled into Joe's Bike Shop. It's an old shop, in an older house, on one of the oldest thoroughfares in Baltimore, but you'd never know by looking at all the carbon fiber, titanium, and high-tech shiny things on display everywhere.

Dave wheeled his bike right up to the work stand of one of the mechanics. I strolled around to the rack of trail guides and began to flip through the most dog-eared copy that was for sale.

"Nice bike," the wrench nodded with approval as he clamped the seat tube, wrapped in a clean towel, into the rubber-coated vise grip of the bike stand.

"Yeah," Dave agreed. "My sister got it for me. It's just like hers."

Dave's Training Log — Week 7

Date	Sleep/Wt.	Workout	Notes
Mon	8 hrs/168		
Tue	7 hrs/169	1 hr: moderate pace	Felt great; worked on new bike and made some adjustments; 17 miles
Wed	9 hrs/169		
Thu	8 hrs/168		
Fri	6 hrs/168		
Sat	7 hrs/168	1.5 hrs: zone 4 22 miles	Rode with Marla part of the way; very fast pace! Felt okay
Sun	8 hrs/169		

Total Riding Hours: **2.5**
Total Miles: **39**

Marla's Training Log— Week 7

Date	Sleep/HR/Wt.	Workout	Notes
Mon	10 hrs/50/139	Off	(cleaned basement all day)
Tue	7 hrs/49/140	30 min run: zone 2	Felt okay
		1.5 hr spin: zone 2	Ran errands
Wed	9 hrs/45/140	2.5 hrs: zones 3–4 mtb ride, with many sprints and jumps	Exhausted at night
Thu	8 hrs/49/139	1.5 hrs: zone 2 mellow ride around reservoir	Felt decent
Fri	10 hrs/47/138	1 hr: zone 2	Easy road ride; tired
		30 min run: zone 2	Sluggish
Sat	9 hrs/53/139	1.5 hrs: zones 2–4, big group ride	Turned around early because of fatigued legs
Sun	10 hrs/53/138	2.5 hrs: zones 2–3	Rode up to Dave's but felt run down; tried to keep it slow

Total Hours: **11.5**

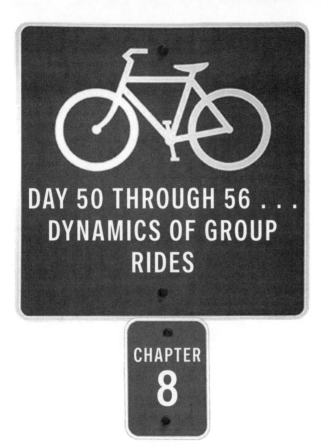

DAY 50 THROUGH 56 . . .
DYNAMICS OF GROUP
RIDES

CHAPTER
8

"Marla," Dave protested in genial big brother tones, "the guy in front is supposed to point and yell out, 'glass!' or something. That way the guy in back who can't see anything anyway knows to watch out for it."

"I know. I know. I just forgot, that's all. I'll change it for you."

"No. That's okay. You don't have to change my tube for me. But it'd be nice if you just gave me a heads-up. That's all."

"I will. I promise." A Hummer zoomed by. Boy, they're loud. Must be the shape or something, but it sounded like a 747 on a landing approach. I wonder if a scoop on the rear of the roof would make a difference.

"Instead of bunny-hopping over it," Dave was saying. He hunched over his front wheel and flipped open his quick-release lever. Down the road in the distance I could still see the twinkling patch of glass.

He stood up and reached back into his jersey for his plastic tire iron. That patch of glass must be about 3 feet wide. I had easily cleared more than 5 feet with my casual hop.

"This tube already has two patches in it. From other rides with you."

"I'm sorry. I thought that you'd know why I was bunny-hopping."

"Marla, you jump caterpillars. You pop over paint lines on the pavement. You jump over *shadows* from overhead telephone wires. It's great riding with you, but you're turning me into a nervous, twitchy wreck! I didn't know there was a glass patch back there; I thought you were just jumping for joy or whatever."

"Sorry, Dave. I ride most of the time alone or on trails." He was forgiving enough to let me take a few turns pumping up his tire. Rush hour hadn't yet crescendoed, so if we made some good time, we could get outside the rim of suburban tracts and still get a good workout before it got dark. I felt bad. I know it's a big effort for him to get on the bike midweek like this, and I should have known better than to be goofing around. I have a little more time for bike tricks.

Fixing a flat

The tube change had cooled us both down a bit, and it took a while to resume our pace. I thought about what a patient brother Dave had always been. And what a brat I always was. Check that, obviously still am. At least around him. I know that I'm more conscientious when I'm riding with acquaintances than I am with Dave. I'd never bunny-hop over some broken glass if I was on a group ride.

During the loop back, I thought about a lot of stuff. The rest of our ride had been pretty quiet.

Side by side as we neared the corner where he turned off, I asked, "Hey, you want to do the Saturday morning Mount Washington group ride?" That ride was a good one. Nice mixture of riders, male and female. Kind of fast pace, but really nice folks. Not snobby or anything like that.

Dave remained quiet, so I enthused, "It's a fun group. You'll like it."

"But," Dave started, "we were supposed to ride Loch Raven. It's in the plan." Dave then passed me as though he wanted to leave me and my suggestion behind.

I shifted gears and caught up. "I know, but this is better. This is a group ride. When we came up with the training plan, I just spaced on group rides. They're fun. And you learn a lot from them. And you just can't stick with the Plan for everything." I winced as I said that.

I knew a big reason why I had been able to convince Dave to go along with a 100-Day Training Plan was because the formalized structure and the rigid continuity of a plan would appeal to his sense of self. Dave is a computer programmer for a reason. He really is comforted by the notion that there is a suitable program for every application. He prides himself on being able to write a good program. Clean and neat and knife-sharp simple. And once a perfectly suitable program is up and running, he frowns on adding any patches. That's one of the reasons he's able to successfully work from home, where so many people find the distractions and interruptions of the daily household emergencies untenable. He's worked hard at smoothing out the home office irregularities of barking dogs, whining leaf blowers, and intruding meter readers. Dave plans out his day in 15-minute increments on his electronic planner. And he sticks to it. I knew that going in.

Without really knowing why at first, I kept our wheels even and maintained a steady pressure. Then things sort of clicked—a reflex whose hardwiring hadn't fired in a long time kicked in. That's how I got my way when we were kids. Dave needs personal space in which to operate. Crowd him, and he'll cave in.

On summer afternoons at the beach in Ocean City, my three older brothers each staked out on the sand an invisible post on which they stood. The program of their game was to throw the Frisbee so accurately that no one need move a leg in order to catch it, and thereby mysteriously attract the attentions of sunbathing girls. If I, scrawny and bucktoothed in a lime green two-piece, wanted to be included in their Frisbee throwing, I knew the way to get a turn was to wrap myself around one of my brother's waists, grab an arm, hang on to a leg so that he couldn't make a good throw. Dave, of all my brothers, believed there was a right way and a wrong way to do things. And that included throwing a Frisbee. John was capable of swatting me to the sand and then ignoring my wailing cries. Moreover, John, being the biggest, didn't care so much for accuracy as he enjoyed hurtling the Frisbee so hard and fast that it bruised and bent back the fingers to catch it. The more I pestered John, the harder he rifled the Frisbee at the heads of his brothers. Mark confidently immobilized me at arm's length by grabbing me with one hand around the back of my skinny neck and squeezing until I closed my eyes and stood on tiptoes quietly still. He didn't mind if I caused one or two of his throws to be off the mark; he knew he'd quickly be able to make an adequate adjustment with a flick of his wrist.

However, Dave, as we all knew, had already perfected the ultimate Frisbee throw. He practiced zipping the Frisbee at the lifeguard stands, at the fence posts that held back the dunes, and at unleashed dogs who patrolled the shores in search of unwary seagulls. Dave took great satisfaction in his aim. He unfailingly hit the bull's-eye of either of my brothers' midsections no matter the distance, regardless of the sea breeze. But Dave could not contend with me nipping at his heels as he threw. I didn't even have to hang on to one of his legs or wrap my arms around his waist. All I had to do was stand really close, right inside his shadow. Just my presence disrupted the smooth flow of his throwing form, and his Frisbee would arc wildly off course, and John and Mark would jeer him. Their taunting voices would carry far up and down the beach, which was dotted thickly by the blankets of sunbathing teenage girls. Dave would really resent that I was throwing him off his game. The exertions of thrusting out his chin and gritting his teeth would skew his Frisbee's trajectory even more. I'd just stand an inch closer. John's deep guffaws would boom across the sands. Mark, whose younger voice hadn't broken yet, would chirp mercilessly that Dave had an arm like a girl. If I shadowed Dave long enough, he would ultimately give in and grant me the occasional chance to cast off a warbly, wobbly Frisbee toss. Or two. Until I was bored enough and afterward decided it would be more fun to stomp up the elaborate sand castle my little brother, Chris, had been painstakingly sculpting for hours at the water's edge.

All I had to do was ride really close to him. So close that our pedals almost touched and our bars almost tangled.

I swung left a little, rewarding him with the space that comforted him so much. Then I allowed him a half-wheel lead to make him feel dominant.

"Dave, you'll like riding with a big group. On those rides everybody is real careful to do everything right. It's a lot of fun, taking pulls and sprinting for hill tops. You go really fast, too. Besides, I think you're getting a little fed up just riding with me. A Century Ride usually draws about a thousand riders, so you'll have to learn how to mix it up with a big group. For hours. All day."

Dave and I have benefited from riding with each other. Commuting and riding with him, I have put more road miles under my wheel than I have since my first season as a pro. And Dave has built a solid base of riding fitness eclipsed only by the six-pack abs of his college days. (He went to college a long time ago, before there was MTV.) Riding together has helped each of us.

Maybe you aren't sure which you like the best, the riding or your partner. It can get blurry. Does the magic of the bike ride make your training partner seem more funny than otherwise? Would your riding partner be as humorous, as insightful, as sensitive, whatever, if he were leaning over the aluminum-framed and beige-upholstered half wall of a cubicle at work? And that person becomes a better friend because of the camaraderie shared during all those cold mornings and blazing hot afternoons. Each joke is funny. Every afternoon golden. And it is challenging to keep up with, or rewarding to pull along, your riding buddy. You find little quirks cute, like your training partner's need to go to the bathroom after each sip from a water bottle. For a while.

Recognize the signs. Out on the road, miles from anybody who can save you when you hear your training buddy start to sing, "Well I gotta mule an'er name is Sal. Fifteen miles on the Erie canal!" remember when you thought the song was funny? But now after a few weeks of riding, you realize that your training partner has a limited repertoire of late 19th-century folk songs. You might want to explore some other riding options.

Every relationship can benefit from some time away from each other. It's not cheating. There is no betrayal or disloyalty. And your riding will benefit as well if you challenge your training by riding at the tempo, distances, and hills of some new people. It's a good idea to mix it up.

It wasn't that Dave was scared or anything. He's not agoraphobic, or a not strong enough rider. I knew what bothered Dave the most about group rides was the politics and mysterious etiquette. The hassles of riding at somebody else's pace. But I also knew that he'd go with us on Saturday. Ultimately, Dave is always up for a challenge.

Group rides are all about politics, or how a group organizes itself. During a group ride, the organization is often unclear, always changing, and random. A group ride is almost the antithesis of a computer program, which Dave admires so deeply.

A group ride will definitely spice up your training plan, but it is excellent training. You won't stick to your planned intervals, stay in your intended zone, or even ride for your target time or distance when you're riding with a group. You can try, but the group, as you will find out, makes its own selections.

Pulling, passing, pacelining, and pointing out dangers are all polite practices that can only be learned in a peloton. Nobody can practice that stuff when training by themselves, and we all get lazy when we ride alone or with the same people week after week. A huge part of being able to ride a Century is learning how to ride with a group. Even though you might imagine that bike riding is inherently solitary, riding in a Century is also very much a complex and chaotic social pursuit.

Cycling can be a solitary effort like rock climbing. You against gravity and the slope. Very simple. Rock climb with a friend and all of a sudden each can belay for the other. You can climb more technical stuff. Like road riding with a training partner, each drafting at times off the other, enabling you to go farther and faster. In each case a bond develops based on trust, empathy, candor, coexistence, and cooperation.

Riding with a large group changes your ride. Transforms it into something other than just a physical activity like working out in the gym. The group changes the solo activity of bike riding into the social sport of bike racing. There is no other sport like it in intensity, strategy, and self-reward.

A group ride is a chaotic affair. It's always moving from an ordered state to a disordered state, and then back to an ordered state. Fractally speaking.

When you show up at a bike shop's parking lot or in front of a coffee shop where most group rides begin, you will probably know who the alpha rider is. It may even be you. Nevertheless, there will be one rider who is the top dog. Most of the time, there is no formal acknowledgment of the strongest rider. He or she won't be wearing a yellow jersey, for instance. The signs will be more subtle. But they are there if you know how to look for them.

1. Look for the one rider whose preride jokes get the most laughs from the group. Even if the punch lines seem lame. That rider is most likely the leader.

2. The leader will be the one who finishes his cup of coffee the most leisurely. When he's done, it's time to go.

3. The leader will be the one confidently answering timorous questions about the proposed route, the possibility of rain, and the likelihood of rising interest rates.

4. Most noticeably, the leader will be the one who signals the start of the ride by clicking in and flaring his nostrils.

That is the ordered state of a group ride. It begins with the unspoken acknowledgment that a group leader exists, the one mighty and strong who shall lead them.

The disordered state will evidence itself almost immediately as the group, once out on the road, formerly pliant and passive, submissive and subdued, plots to do in the leader. For the rest of the ride, if the group has any spine at all, it will try its best to stab their leader in the back. The group, like a pack of wild hyenas, will prod and probe for any weakness the leader may exhibit. If the leader exposes for an instant the soft underbelly of a gimpy cadence, the group will turn on him and rip him to shreds. It's not always great to be the leader.

By the end of the ride, either the leader will have reasserted his dominance, or a new leader will have emerged, and an ordered state will return. About the only benefit conferred on a leader is that somebody else might buy you a beer after the ride. Sometimes that's enough status to reward the effort. This stasis will be maintained until next week's ride, when the cycle will repeat itself.

As you can see, the social science of a group ride can be very messy. That's why Dave would rather wash his hands of the whole mess. But I think the experience and insights gained from group rides are only outmatched by the fun.

During a group ride, you simply cannot try to lead from start to finish. I've learned that the hard way. On your first time out with a group, tend toward the rear until you know you have enough to hang on until the end of the ride. More important than leading the ride for any length of time is the ability to finish the whole ride. Take your pulls in turn as they come to you, but be sure not to overwork yourself. The group will appreciate a modest effort, but if the pace appreciably slows every time you're pulling, the group would appreciate it more if you keep your turn at the front short.

When road riding with a group, there is simply no reason to beat any other single individual, one-on-one, not even the leader. It's not a *mano a mano* sport like boxing or Ping-Pong where the play is defined by the close interaction with your opponent: Move and countermove. Advantage is not gained by a solitary act of heroic achievement unless you want to attack on every climb to gloat at every summit.

The solo breakaway rider makes his effort, the success of which is dependent on the peloton's response. The solo breakaway rider is more often at the mercy of the group, not at the mercy of an individual. It can pursue or sit tight. Very seldom does a road racer's solo breakaway at the sound of the start gun last until the finish. The group can choose to let the breakaway run out of steam all by itself, or it can choose to actively chase it down. Through the power of pacelining, rotating a strong, fresh rider at the lead every few minutes, the peloton can quickly chase down almost any solo breakaway rider. The group's strength is actually enhanced by the air pressure it creates by its own movement down the road.

It sounds unbelievable, but any rider, a group even more so, disturbs the air as it moves through it. Some of this air takes the form of resistance and friction, which the rider must overcome, but some of this air curls around behind and rushes to fill in the space the rider formerly occupied. This air that rushes in to fill the "empty" space behind a rider exerts a push, which increases the force of forward momentum. It's been found that riding behind someone is 30 percent easier, because of decreased air pressure. This effect is greatly exaggerated by a large group riding quickly.

In a fun group ride, or a racing peloton, the interplay between the riders determines the leader or the winner at the end of the day.

On a road ride, each rider must choose from countless possible options the best response to a myriad of situations. And the group makes its own selections as well. Failure to chase down an attack, respond to a tempo change, or acknowledge which rider has some strength in store for a sprint, or setting a pace too high can negate all of your strategy and cut off at the knees any chance at a win. In a road race like the Tour de France, it is accepted wisdom that the strongest sprinter, the best climber, the fastest time-trialer, the leader of the best team all are subject to external events like weather, a dog crossing the course, the desertion of a domestique, a crash of the peloton, some stomach-rattling cheese, or the interplay of all these components. From all this chaotic interplay, one rider always, choosing from all the options, responds in the best way and emerges as the winner.

Though arriving at a winner in road racing is dependent on the interplay among all the riders in the group, the social interaction between the racers is not nearly so static as that found in other sports. Positions don't change in partner pursuits like the two-man bobsled, in which success depends on a pusher working with a driver as a team, opposing other teams. Imagine, if during the middle of your bobsled run, your pusher decides to switch alliances, and he drops his foot outside the sled and digs his heel into the snow, slowing you down on purpose. It would be scandalous!

That can happen during a road race. In road cycling, even on a team, one can ride for oneself even against those on his own team. It's widely understood and accepted. Greg Lemond famously opted to ride on the final stage for the Tour de France win by himself, instead of riding as a team member for his team leader, Bernard Hinault. During a road race, many alliances may team up, spontaneously, temporarily, duplicitously, and grudgingly. These may be alliances between two individual riders from separate teams. Or it may be between whole teams. Or combinations of teams and disparate riders all reasoning that they have a tactical mutual benefit in working together, even if it's to prevent yet another rider from winning.

I think that cycling in a group has no comparison to any other sport. It's like playing chess on multiple imaginary boards in your head, memorizing each piece's relative location, weighing every potential move against unseen opponents while simultaneously playing poker with cheaters in the peloton, betting, anteing up, drawing, bluffing, looking for a tell, sitting tight, folding, and either getting busted or winning the pot, except the whole time your legs are pedaling like crazy, and you can't breathe, empty your bladder, or take a sip of water. Meanwhile, you must convince the other riders you feel great.

Dave did pretty well his first time out with a big group. He followed the three big rules of preparation.

1. He made sure his bike was ready for the ride. Even though every-body is very nice, nobody really enjoys having to stop to adjust your rear derailleur throughout the ride.

2. He was self-sufficient. Full water bottles, quick tool, patch, pump, tube, and a little bit of cash for precoffee and postbeer.

3. He did not talk too much smack in the parking lot prior to the ride.

Here are some other tips if you want to get into some of these groups.

1. When you first meet everybody in the parking lot, repeat their names over and over to yourself, until you know everyone. It can be a real drag riding for hours with nice people whom you can't call by name.

2. If you have business cards, bring 'em. But don't hand any out until after the ride, and then only if someone asks for a way to contact you about another upcoming ride. I forget cards a lot, and few people carry pens in their chamois.

3. It's all in fun. If you can't hang on, it's nothing personal. Even now, if I get dropped on a group ride, I don't worry about it. I just figure I'll stick it out longer next time.

Dave's Training Log— Week 8

Date	Sleep/Wt.	Workout	Notes
Mon	9 hrs/169		
Tue	7 hrs/168		
Wed	6 hrs/168	1.5 hrs: easy pace, 24 miles	
Thu	9 hrs/168		
Fri	8 hrs/167		
Sat	7 hrs/166	1.5 hrs	Tried to ride easy, but went mod a few times on climbs; first big group ride; great drafting! Peeled off early
Sun	8 hrs/169		

Total Riding Hours: **3**
Total Miles: **51**

Marla's Training Log— Week 8

Date	Sleep/HR/Wt.	Workout	Notes
Mon	9 hrs/47/137	1 hr gym, upper body only (with 30 min warmup on stair climber)	
Tue	10 hrs/45/139	1 hr: zone 2	Easy ride with Dave
		30 min run: zone 2	Good
Wed	8 hrs/44/139	1.5 hrs: zones 3–5 on BMX bike on race track	Practiced manuals; good legs
Thu	7 hrs/NA/139		Off (packed for travel)
Fri	8 hrs/46/NA	2 hrs: zones 2–3	Not much energy; too much snow on roads; good film shoot
Sat	7 hrs/NA/NA	2 hrs: zones 3–4	Big group ride; feeling better
Sun	9 hrs/53/NA	30 min: zone 2	Raced time trial in cold rain; couldn't warm up or cool down because of logistics

Total Hours: **8.5**

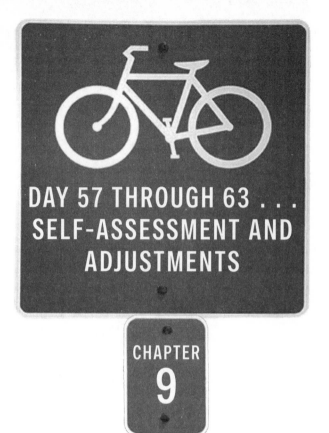

DAY 57 THROUGH 63 . . . SELF-ASSESSMENT AND ADJUSTMENTS

CHAPTER
9

Perkiness doesn't come naturally to me. Dave's plan called for a 50-mile ride today. We didn't have that much farther to go, but to get over this hump, our ride needed a jolt of something. So I put on a sort of perky, "You're more than halfway through your 100-Day Century Ride Training Plan!"

"I'm aware of that. I was the one who spreadsheeted it, remember?"

"Yesss," I shusshed back, "I know. Doesn't do me any good. I can't open them up on my iBook." Today I had nothing in my legs. Just full of cement. Could have whacked my kneecaps with a hammer and felt nothing.

"Macs are for kids. Grow up."

Right now I wasn't feeling so chipper. So for that last crack of his, I just decided to drop him for a while. At least for a good 5 minutes. Maybe 10. I shifted all the way down on my cog set so that I was in my biggest gear. My legs had no zip, but I can always count on my ability to grind and mash beyond the point of sensible sensation.

I love my iBook. On it I can watch DVDs. Do all my business. I log all my music into it, which makes it easy to keep my iPod fresh. True, I get some files from e-mails that I can't open with my iBook. Nobody can read the stuff that I send them, because the indents are all off, the boldface missing, and the punctuation screwed up. Forget about photos. Dave is right in a way. It's tough living in a Windows world.

Dave is supposed to ride the 50 miles today the way he expects to ride during his Century . . . warm up during the first few miles and then slip into zone 2 for the long stretch. Be able to respond well during the climbs. If he's feeling good, bring it home the last half of the ride in zone 3 with bursts of zone 4 if he thinks he can win some draft beer primes. Dave should be able to comfortably and confidently ride the second half of today's 50 miles at a faster clip than the first. That's a negative split. He should be finishing strong, feeling like he could do it all over again after just refilling his water bottle with some Gatorade and grabbing a Clif Bar.

The reality of my ride today was more like 100 miles and change, when the commute back to the city is added in. The 50 miles in the middle was just supposed to be saddle time. I planned on pulling Dave most of the way. Pulling him along was part of my workout. Zones 3 and 4. I know, not a very scientific training technique, but sometimes you have to concede bike riding is very elemental. Training to ride for long distances requires that you sometimes ride for long distances. After the meat of the ride, I could handle a cooldown the length of Charles Street all the way to the harbor and home. I didn't mind the road time. I have always enjoyed a good long ride.

But I just wasn't enjoying the time with him today.

Dave wasn't trying to be smart-alecky when he made that comment about growing up. I'm sure he was smirking when he said it. It's just hard to read a human expression from a butt's-eye view. It's probably nothing, probably just me.

As we got closer to Dave's wide-lawned neighborhood, I slowed down, much to his obvious relief. Gave him a breather on my wheel for a while. His "grow up" comment was left back there on the road somewhere. Not important now. I knew anyway that I didn't have much in me for the ride home. I knew I'd make it, but just end up overdoing it. Too ambitious today.

We wheeled around the corner of his street, and I let him lead out. A small consideration. His kids might be watching. Can't be a good thing for any dad's kids to see their aunt dragging their father home by a bike length. Dave's street is wide from curb to curb. And quiet. The cars stay on the driveways, and the kids stay in the yards. The houses are all set back behind huge leafy bushes.

I could hear the dog, Jed, barking from inside the house. Lorena must have taken the boys somewhere, because there was no car in the driveway. They're always going somewhere, it seems. Some kind of camp or something. I don't know how Dave and Lorena manage the kids' schedules on top of their own.

We leaned the bikes along the vinyl siding of the house. Dave sighed the tiniest bit. He hated that vinyl siding. Wanted in the worst way to strip it off. He usually told me so every time we leaned our bikes against it. Maybe replace it with cedar shingle, he'd say. Or redwood clapboard. Something like that. It changes. But today he was just tired, so the sigh was all he could manage.

The deck was Dave's home improvement project from last year. The two steps up to it aren't a big deal, but it's a long walk across it to the Adirondack chair where I plop down. Dave slides open the glass door, and the dog explodes from the kitchen.

Too much energy.

Dave goes in and comes back out with some fruit, chips, and two bottles of beer. I have the good chair. The one where you can rest your feet on the part that slides out. He slumps down into the other one, the small of his back bent in an arch bridging from the chair seat to the chair back. His big feet are crammed close to the chair's legs, making his bony knees stick up high and out, and his arms don't have the good angle for the armrests. I have the good angle. I stretch my arms out on the sun-warmed wood.

While we sip our beers, Jed sniffs out a ride report from our chamois and from our shoes. Where have we been? Past whose telephone poles, mailboxes, and curbs have we ridden? I see. Ah yes, that roadkill on top of Bottom Road is decomposing nicely. Spilled some Endurox on our shoes today, did we? Messy. That bitch of a Weimaraner chased us nipping at our heels again, did she? Hmmph.

I'm sure Jed's cold doggy nose assessment of our ride is as accurate as our own.

Shouldn't have accepted the beer. I leave it unsipped on the armrest. I am really thirsty but too lazy to stand up and walk to the bathroom. "Dave, you should grab the notebook so we can check it out."

He wasn't looking too comfortable in his chair anyway. As he disappears into the kitchen, I yell after him, "And some water, please!"

I have 25 more miles to get home. And no iPod. It's my own fault for not fully charging it, though. Let that be my punishment for overdoing it. I don't need to look at my training plan to confirm that. My legs have been telling me that all day. All week practically. I think I'm overtraining.

I'm always tired, but I can't sleep. For the last week or so, I wink out when watching a DVD. Eventually, I brush my teeth and crawl back into bed, but I just lay there wide awake. Elevated heart rate when I wake in the morning, but then I can't get my heart rate up past 170 when I'm riding. No appetite, no flavor in my food, and I've been picking through Marc's delicious cooking like it's a prison plate.

The purpose of today's ride was supposed to be a test of how Dave's training has been going. It was supposed to be a halfway-point checkup, like a midsemester test, to see if he has been naughty or nice in sticking to his training plan. I figured there was a pretty good chance that he'd be off a bit. This 50-miler would provide an indication how much. That way we could make some adjustments to get him back on track.

I didn't really think that I'd be guilty of being off track, too.

Because Dave was training for his first Century Ride, and because the first time you do anything it's very hard, I had anticipated that he'd be a little behind in his conditioning. Because he's so busy. His own small business. Lorena with hers. The boys, the dog, the house. Just life. Hard to squeeze in a bike ride a few times a week.

And, I was right. He's been missing some of his rides and not making up for them on his off days. I could tell around halfway today that he didn't have it in him. He started out okay. He was strong on the hills. Stayed right with me on the flats, but just around 1½ hours, where you normally expect a little bonk if you don't eat, he had a big one. A bonk is when the body has exhausted its glycogen stores; the tank goes empty. It happens. If you've been training the right way, your body should be able to rebound from that dip in energy simply by topping off your tank. Eating a Fig Newton, squeezing in a couple of Clif shots. Downing an Accelerade energy drink. You just have to keep hydrating and putting in the carbs. That'll usually do it. But it won't be enough if you haven't been riding enough.

Dave's bonk wasn't a surprise. A little tweaking to his program shouldn't be a big deal. Plenty of time to go before his big day. He was already looking better now that he was eating.

I figured I would just fire him up a little. Pep talk. Juggle some stuff in his schedule so he could ride just a little more next week. And the week after, up his intensity a notch, and Dave would be fine. Obviously, he's strong enough to finish a Century Ride, but I know that 100 miles seems a little daunting. Remind him of the big picture. He wants to kick Chris's butt. Perfectly expressed as Dave finally burst out laughing, "I'm going to kick Chris's butt!" So there it was.

Our little brother, 10 years Dave's junior, has been talking a lot of smack lately. Not proper outright trash talk. More like the annoying comments. Chris is only 34 years old. No kids, no hassles. He's an engineer and consultant who sets his own hours. Last summer he spontaneously sea kayaked in Alaska for 6 weeks. Lives in the city a block from Marc and me renting a row house with another bachelor guy. Both of them score tickets for Orioles games on a regular basis. Chris looks like he's still in school. Weighs the same he did when he graduated, in fact. He's dating girls who still *are* in school. Chris zips around town on his skateboard from Whole Foods to happy hour at the Rope Walk. Occasionally he hops on his titanium-framed, Rolf-wheeled, carbon-forked, Italian leather—saddled, too-cool-for-decals road bike to mom and dad's house on a midweek morning at a whim. Pick up some mail, take a nap in the den, and then ride home again before it gets dark.

All this gets under Dave's skin just a tad.

Lately, Chris casually says stuff like, "You know, I've been thinking. It might be fun to do that Century Ride with you guys. When is it again? Oh, that's right after I come back from my trip to Machu Pichu. But no worries." I know it sets Dave on edge.

Because what Chris says is true. It's no worry for him to ride 100 miles a few days after coming back from a month-long trip to the Andes. Chris is one of those guys who could still put on his high-school cross-country uniform and run the old loop, faster.

Even if Dave was behind in his training, all I had to do to get him fired up to ride his bike a little more was to remind him that Chris said 100 miles would be, "No problem." Dave would type into his planner, "Crush Chris!" and the next hour he was on his bike Dave would be ahead of Moser's pace.

That's how brothers show their love for one another. Each, in their own way, making the other guy suffer. Dave carried from the kitchen two water bottles, two cold slices of pizza that had been delivered the night before, and his training logbook. Looking at the pizza made my stomach queasy. But I ate it anyway while we flipped through the last couple pages in his book.

The pizza tasted okay at first while I was chewing it, but it didn't settle well. I kept trying to burp while Dave equivocated about why he had been slacking about putting in his saddle time. I didn't really pay close attention. I knew he had good reasons why he had cut short some rides the last couple of weeks. This Century Ride stuff was supposed to be a fun thing for him. He already had plenty of work. Months ago, I had told him we'd be riding together all the time, and how great it'd be. And fun. Lately I'd blown off a lot of our rides. I'm sure it curbed his enthusiasm somewhat to listen to a voice message from me telling him that I was going out of town for a few days to do a photo shoot and some riding in Colorado. Or that I was disappearing to train in West Virginia.

Pros can do that. Pros can always go for rides. But pros shouldn't be overtraining. That's even more of a rookie mistake than not training enough, because pros should know better.

Self-Assessment

As far as your training plan goes, this is the fat part of the bell curve. All the real work should be done right now and continue on for the next few weeks before you start to taper off. If this is your first Century Ride, this is the period where you should be putting in the most miles on the bike. If you have set a goal of finishing your Century in under 6 hours, or if you want to win your class, or if you're going for the overall win, right now is the critical stage of your training. If you're just planning on riding some Centuries as a training method for other cycling goals that you may have, such as 24-hour races or an enjoyable cycling tour across France, the miles that you ride now will make those miles easier. If you hope to do more than just complete your Century Ride without a life-lift helicopter hovering over you as you roll under the finish-line banner, you should be able to ride 50 miles easily.

So you've just finished a 50-miler, so how do you feel? You think you are where you should be?

Has your training log matched your ideal plan? Or are there a lot of empty spaces in your log? Does that mean you have been riding as you should, but you're just not great at keeping records? How many hours have you been riding? Are you where you thought you'd be at this point?

The training plan is built around the premise of two or three rides on weekdays with one longer ride during the weekend. Have you been looking for time to ride rather than making time to ride? Have there been too many 1-hour riding sessions and not enough 2-hour rides during the last few weeks?

What about the weekends? Have you been good during the week but bad during the weekends, neglecting those long rides?

There will always be differences between your ideal training plan and your actual training plan, but how great have the differences been trending? Don't worry too much; a couple of weeks of falling short of your ideal training targets will not completely derail you. After all, you just finished a 50-miler, didn't you? You are going to be able to do your Century Ride, that is a definite. Even if you flatline your training curve from here on out, missing all your future training targets, you'll more than likely have enough in you to tough out your Century. But perhaps you want more than that.

Thumb back through your training plan to the first few pages and look at your original goals.

Look at the figures you came up with when you determined your baseline fitness level. Is your weight the same? Have the number of your pushups and situps plateaued? Re-establish your baseline from this point. Compare where you are now to how you were before you started training. Are you satisfied?

Minor Adjustments

Here are a few basic ways that you could find yourself off track.

1. Your training has been lacking.

2. You have been training too much.

3. Your goals weren't realistic.

There are three ways that your training can be lacking. Either you haven't been riding enough, you haven't been riding long enough, or you haven't been riding hard enough. The first two are easier to check for. Consult your training plan, and look it up. If you have been riding your bike with enough frequency and duration, sticking with a reasonable diet, and getting your sleep, the reason that you didn't decisively finish your 50-miler may be that you didn't monitor the intensity of your rides.

A heart rate monitor can be expensive and a bit of a pain, and it is understandable if you didn't purchase one when you first started training. Although a good technique, watching your Rate of Perceived Exertion is not as accurate. Who wants to go out and buy every gizmo all at once whenever you start with a new sport? Since you have made it this far, though, you should start thinking of a heart rate monitor as a wise investment. An HR monitor can be a safeguard against wasted effort or junk miles. Besides, a heart rate monitor is cheaper than a PowerTap, a much discussed piece of equipment used to watch your power output.

The intensity zones are keys to improvement. If you want to ride with a gadget, trade in that MP3 player for a heart rate monitor. You'll quickly see how much more effective its beeps are at keeping you within your targeted intensity zones.

Sometimes it's hard to train intensely while riding alone, even with a heart rate monitor. Even if you just buddy up with a training partner once a week, or if you can latch on with a group for long weekend rides, you may see your intensity levels perk up from the competition and camaraderie.

And there are times when your training partner may just be slowing you down. The mellow group may be a lot of fun to ride with on Sunday mornings but may be the wrong group to train with to achieve your goals. You might have to search around for faster riders to team up with or consider steeling yourself for the discipline of riding solo with an HR monitor.

You may be one of those people who only puts out the truly intense efforts when a race is on the line. The old adage that racing is the best training is quite true. If you find that your fitness has plateaued, your riding buddies can't light a fire in your gut, and spending the money for a heart rate monitor does not enthrall you, then you should think about signing up for some local races. If the intensity of the race scene doesn't square with your health insurance deductible, you might find it more economical to throw down for a PowerTap after all.

If you're sure that your training rides haven't been lacking in frequency, duration, or intensity, then you should re-examine your original goal. Was your goal unrealistic to begin with?

Is your goal simply beyond your reach? That's very common. Did you really plan on setting the all-time record for your Century Ride? Surprised that after today's 50-miler you're not quite at a record-setting pace? Recovering from the emotional crash of an unmet goal is entirely preventable. Re-examine your goal based on some measure of reality. You have been riding with some other people; what are their goals? Is your goal in line with theirs? Have you been hitting your daily training goals? If not, do you really think you can achieve your overall goal? Have you set for yourself a goal that is not even measurable by any objective standards? Don't laugh, but was your goal to ride your bike to look cool?

As it turned out, I myself was off track of my periodized training. During that 50-miler with Dave, I realized that I had lost my training focus. I had been trying to do too much, and more important, not taking the proper rest. Ninety-nine percent of the time overtraining results from an imbalance between training and recovery. One should remember the 3 to 1 training/recovery ratio. An increase in training intensity requires a commensurate increase in recovery. For me the easy answer for almost everything is to go for a ride. Do I want to improve my top end speed? Go for a ride. Feel like I ate too much over the holiday weekend? Go for a ride. Worried about the cost of homeowner's insurance? Go for a ride. Feeling that my training isn't going well? Go for a ride. Do you see a pattern here?

Ways of Overtraining

1. Routine and repetitious nature of your rides, with the same distance, intensity, route, etc., for weeks at a time

2. Too much racing weekend after weekend and working out too hard in between without the proper recovery

3. Continuing to train at high intensity through minor colds or allergies or during bad weather

4. Neglecting nutritional needs as you increase your training intensities

5. Outside sources of stress, such as problems at work or school, or relationship meltdowns, can be just enough to push you over the edge. Riders often use their workouts as a way to reduce emotional or psychological stress levels, but may find themselves overwhelmed if outside stress becomes too great.

Adjusting your training plan because you may be overtrained requires some subtlety and patience.

First of all, be sure of the cause of your sub par 50-miler. There is a difference between being Overtrained with a capital O, and overtraining with a small o. Being Overtrained is much more serious and much more difficult to deal with. Whereas overtraining is usually not such a big deal and can be more easily remedied.

Being Overtrained means that you have systematically run your body through hard workouts with insufficient recovery to the point where now there is not much you can do about it except stay off your bike. Sometimes in severe cases, that can mean for the entire season. That alone can be very stressful for serious cyclists, which only makes matters worse. It's a vicious cycle.

Few Americans have access to such specialized health care as sports medicine in order to get a diagnosis of being Overtrained. Not that many club coaches can even make such a determination definitively, and most clubs don't have a club doctor. After the fact, when you're laid up in bed with mononucleosis, Epstein-Barr viral syndrome, or chronic fatigue syndrome, it's pretty easy to see you were Overtrained. But prior to then, a self-assessment is very subjective.

This is one of the reasons that your training plan is so important. If you haven't been filling it out on a daily basis, you are pretty screwed, since there is no way to go back now to check to see what your resting heart rate or hours of sleep were 4 weeks ago.

Signs of Overtraining

1. Elevated waking heart rate, difficulty hitting your target heart rate while riding, or inability to ride for sustained periods at your anaerobic threshold (zone 4)

2. Swollen lymph nodes under the arms and neck

3. Decreased sex drive

4. General lethargy, pervasive achiness, and irritability

5. Fitful sleep, loss of appetite, and lack of attention span

Are you now riding more miles than at this time last year? More than 30 percent? You might be overtraining.

Now what to do?

I know it will drive you crazy if I simply say to stay off the bike for a while. After all, you are right smack in the middle of the road to your Century. All your competition is racking up the miles, right now! They're getting stronger every day. Leaner every time out on the road. All those training miles that you worked so hard to put in will be in vain if you abandon your training now. Might as well write the whole season off right now. Let the hair on your legs grow out. Why bother with the whole thing? Next year you'll be forgotten, and all those riders who passed you by this year will be fighting for your spot in the peloton. Sponsors won't return your calls. Nobody will be buying you any cups of fat-free mocha cappuccino with extra foam on the side in another cup next season.

Sound melodramatic?

Okay, it is.

However, if you find that you are Overtrained, the best thing to do is get off the bike for a while, take walks instead, and monitor your overall health for positive signs of recovery. The best way to see if you're recovering is by systematically checking your waking heart rate to see if it drops to the normal level. So, even though you might not be riding at this point, you are still in training. It's important to keep that mind-set. You must be as hard working and even more diligent during your recovery than you were during the rides that led up to your being Overtrained in the first place.

If you are Overtrained with a capital O:

- Going completely cold turkey and not riding your bike for weeks will drive you crazy. So you can ride a couple times a week, but only a half hour at a time, in zone 1, and ignore anybody riding past you. You must stick with your "recovery workout."

- Take up some other physical activity that's less intense, such as hiking, golf, or yard work. But resist the urge to turn this activity into a training session.

- Maintain a healthy diet appropriate to your reduced caloric output, so when you do get back on your bike, you won't have to work so hard sweating off some extra pounds.

- After your waking heart rate returns to normal levels, you can gradually up your duration and intensity.

- Full recovery may take as long as 8 to 12 weeks.

If I feel that I am simply overtraining with a small o:

- I completely break my bike down and look for where that creaking noise is coming from. That usually takes a couple of days. Then I can resume riding, but at intensities and durations somewhat lower than I had been.

- I go onto our sailboat or to my mom's house and just hang out for a couple of days. I get my taxes done early, put all those shoe boxes of photos into some albums, coordinate all the blinking lights on the microwave, DVD player, and coffee machine to the same time. Then I can resume riding, but at intensities and durations somewhat lower than I had been.

- Mix up my riding. If I've been training on the road, I go for some *easy* dirt rides or vice versa. Then I can resume riding, but at intensities and durations somewhat lower than I had been.

• Ride for several days with Marc, who is confoundingly slow. Then I can resume riding, but at intensities and durations somewhat lower than I had been.

Notice any patterns?

When I feel better, I resume training where I left off.

Dave's Training Log— Week 9

Date	Sleep/Wt.	Workout	Notes
Mon	7 hrs/169		
Tue	8 hrs/168		
Wed	8 hrs/168		(No time to ride!)
Thu	9.5 hrs/168		
Fri	5 hrs/167		
Sat	8 hrs/166	3 hrs: Rode 49 miles on test ride to check out progress	Thought I felt okay at first, but bonked at end. Bummer.
Sun	8 hrs/166		

Total Riding Hours: **3**
Total Miles: **49**

Marla's Training Log— Week 9

Date	Sleep/HR/Wt.	Workout	Notes
Mon	9 hrs/45/137	1.5 hr run with some walking	Felt okay
Tue	7 hrs/48/138	2.5 hrs: zone 2	Felt recovered
Wed	7 hrs/49/139	3 hrs: zones 2–4	Mtb ride with photo shoot; lots of sprinting and hill repeats
Thu	7 hrs/45/140	30 min: zone 1	Easy spin to gym
		30 min in gym	Easy upper body
Fri	9 hrs/43/139		Off
Sat	7 hrs/48/139	5 hrs: zones 2–3	Rode out to Dave's then pushed him up and down the hills; felt horrible, legs trashed
Sun	9 hrs/49/141	30 min: zone 2 hike	
Total Hours: **13.5**			

DAY 64 THROUGH 70 . . . STRENGTHENING YOUR BASE

CHAPTER 10

Dave has never let me drive his Audi before. He doesn't even like the thought that guys at the dealership drive it into the repair bay for its regular tune-ups. The only person other than himself allowed behind the wheel is Lorena. She's a more aggressive driver anyway, better suited for the Audi's robust powertrain. But the Audi was mine to command for a couple of hours. So as I squeezed the leather wheel through the curves, I felt quite honored. Marc was holding a newspaper up high in front of his face so that the windshield was completely blocked. The Audi's four wheels drifted across the road's corners. Marc shifted his weight in the seat and rattled his paper loudly. I was being naughty, but I did resist the urge to fiddle with the bass of the car's sound system. Instead of fumbling with his stereo settings, I concentrated on my developing appreciation for the sleek, low-profile Michelins he had mounted not long ago.

This morning Dave had picked us up at our doorstep. He zoomed along the beltway, a map's folds dividing the front seat between Dave and me, with Marc crammed in the back, his legs twisted in knots amid gym bags. We headed out to the Eastern Shore, the long peninsula of wooded marshes, river mouths, and shifting sands which makes up the land on the far side of Chesapeake Bay. As Baltimore mainlanders say, we're going "downy" ocean. The Eastern Shore, sometimes known as the Delmarva Coast because it comprises the seaward side of Delaware, Maryland, and Virginia, stretches more than 100 miles along its oceanfront from Rehoboth Beach in the north to the scattered barrier islands of Chincoteague and Assateague to the south. The inside of the arm, the bay side, appears and disappears with the rising and falling tides of the bay and is anchored solidly to shore by Route 50's Bay Bridge. My mom and dad were lucky enough they say, I say smart enough, to buy a beach house in Bethany Beach years ago before the Eastern Shore started to boom with second homes, strip malls, golf courses, and parking lots. There are still a lot of farms and marshland, though not as much as I remember.

Dave pays the bridge toll, and I press my face to the passenger window glass and from the span's height scan the shoreline. There still lean familiar small, old cottages of oystermen and tidal farmers, which show the bay's muddy high-water marks from winter storms on their chipping whitewashed walls, but I can't see any. I mostly notice the new, great-roomed, executive homes that have elbowed their way onto the shore. They sit on stilts, or atop three-car garages, and are visited only during the summer tourist season anyway. Memorial Day is still a couple of months away, so we have the road all to ourselves. That's the idea. Some empty roads. Incredibly flat roads. For Dave to rack up some miles on his bike.

I am not supposed to be riding. I'm overcooked for this week. If I were a dinner entrée, I would be blackened redfish, perilously close to dry and flaky. A dish like this can only be recovered with a savory sauce that Marc would whip up, like roasted red peppers and caramelized red onions in a reduction of champagne and cream. And so Marc has strongly recommended that I coach Dave for a few days rather than ride myself. That's a tough recipe to swallow.

That's the way it is with overtraining; it's very hard to realize by yourself that it's happening to you. The athlete tends to think that any drop in energy or lack of power or any dip in performance must surely be the result of not enough training. Spouses, unless they're faster than you, tend to be ignored when they suggest training tips or even when they point out what is obvious. "What do you know about it?" is the most typical response given to a spouse who has just pre-scribed the right treatment for you—a couple of days off. Although Marc is a sport-level rider and slow on the bike, I do sometimes listen to him, usually after I've already learned the hard way. He did endure 11 years of competitive swimming, from grade school right through college, so he must have retained a little something about over-training.

So that's why Dave has allowed me to drive his Audi. We plan to drop him off in Dover, on the bay side, and then pick him up again on the ocean side. In exchange, I'm letting him use my heart rate mon-itor. This is his first ride with one. Before the week is over, he'll prob-ably go out and buy one of those fancy downloadable ones so he can play with numbers on his PC. Some people find heart rate monitors annoying; my bet is that Dave will find one appealing. Numbers, pat-terns, and target levels make Dave swoon. I like them, too. They're fun to play with when passing time during a ride.

Dave is enjoying his ride today; I can tell because he didn't even look up when I buzzed his head with the passenger door mirror. He just kept on pedaling. This will be perfect. Just a couple days "downy" ocean for Dave to work out and for me to stay off my bike.

I hope Dave's car can handle it. I know Marc is having a tough time with the G-forces.

High mileage or high intensity? You have to choose one or the other. You really shouldn't train both at the same time. Doing both at the same time is called racing. With a little more than a month and a half to go, Dave is in the period of training where he needs to alternate regularly between both. The training base he creates for himself should be wide and deep so he can draw from it at will during his Century Ride.

Dave had been pretty good about doing his rides and filling out his logs. And I had made sure that at least once a week we had gone for a fairly decent long ride. But I couldn't go on every ride with him to monitor his intensity. Although brilliant conceptually, my original idea to ride with him on my off day had run me down just a little too much. I blame it on that blasted commute.

That's how he ended up wearing my heart rate monitor, and I ended up driving his sweet Audi.

Over the last few nights prior to coming to the Eastern Shore, we had established Dave's intensity zones 1 through 5. We employed the standard formula for determining the maximum heart rate and then took percentages of the max heart rate.

205 minus (Age divided by 2)

Dave is 45 years old. Fairly fit . . . 205 minus 23 (his age divided by 2) equals 182.

Dave's morning heart rate is 60 beats per minute.

Dave's maximum heart rate as derived from the formula is about 182 beats per minute (BPM). The intensity zones are set up as percentages of his maximum heart rate.

MAX HEART RATE: 182 BPM

Zone 1	50 to 60%	91 to 109 BPM
Zone 2	60 to 70%	109 to 127 BPM
Zone 3	70 to 80%	127 to 145 BPM
Zone 4	80 to 90%	145 to 164 BPM
Zone 5	90 to 100%	164 to 182 BPM

Yesterday, he had ridden 1 hour and 30 minutes, but within strict parameters. It was a zones 3 and 4 day for him. His total workout is listed below.

Total Workout Time: 1:30

30 minutes warmup. Start at zone 1 and end at zone 2

10 minutes at zone 3

5 minutes recovery zone 1

10 minutes at zone 4

5 minutes recovery zone 1

30 minutes cooldown zone 1

The riding didn't wipe him out. He's in pretty good shape, after all. The Eastern Shore is flat, flat, flat. I figured that he would be more able to stay within his targeted heart rate zones if he didn't have to deal with even the small hills that Baltimore County can throw at you. I also thought that since he would be learning about the small monitor clipped to his bar, he might not be paying as much attention to the road as he normally would. The roads out here are relatively empty and therefore safer. I didn't want him to be caught off guard because of an approaching car. Even if it was his own. And I didn't want him to get hurt because he was so preoccupied with his new toy, he might inadvertently blow through a stop sign or fail to yield when merging.

But what I did want for Dave was for him to be treated after his ride the way I like to be treated. Though I rarely get the full treatment after a hard workout.

Yesterday Dave rode with high intensity; today he was riding high mileage, 45 miles, but at a *lower* intensity. Today's ride was supposed to help him recover from yesterday's exertions while still adding to his base level of fitness. There is also a psychological element to riding 2 or 3 hours. The more times you can stay in the saddle for those long rides, the more you get used to the idea that such long rides aren't really that hard. To do so, you have to stay focused and not exceed your intensity zone.

Marc and I parked and waited for Dave by the side of the road where a seasonal fruit and vegetable stand normally was set up. This time of year, the stand's windows and doors were shut tight, and the gravel lot closed off with a rusty droop of chain. The liberal voices of NPR eased from Dave's stereo, which was conservatively set on level three. I was flipping through one of my mom's beach house detective novels. Marc crouched outside throwing rocks at squirrels and not hitting any. In a gym bag on the backseat sat a warm set of clean, dry clothes for Dave. There was a plastic box of baby wipes back there, too. Dave's kids are older now, so baby wipes might surprise him. On the floor sitting upright on the rubber mat there cooled a half-gallon of spring water. Beside it there leaned a premixed water bottle of recovery drink. And one beer hidden behind it for Marc.

Outside the car, Marc had our work stand set up on a level patch of loose gravel. At its base were clustered a pail of warm, soapy water, a soft-bristled scrub brush, some clean rags, and various little eye-droppers of lubricant and spray bottles of degreaser.

As Dave skidded to a stop, surprising both of us, we sprang into action. I hit the preset station button, sending the stereo back to Rush Limbaugh land, and Marc grabbed Dave's handlebar. Dave swung his long leg over the top tube and struggled to unbutton the chin strap of his helmet with his wind-chilled fingers. As soon as he removed his helmet, Dave began babbling about his heart rate and how well he had ridden, his bright eyes wide with excitement. Marc had popped Dave's bike into the stand and was already scrubbing the drivetrain with the soapy brush. Dave hopped an awkward dance through the gravel lot, asking if we had seen the way he sliced into that headwind, wanting to know if his back looked as flat as it had felt. A grown man on a bike. What a kid.

I opened the back door of the Audi to give Dave some privacy alongside the desolate road while he stripped out of his chamois and top. He figured out how to use the baby wipes as a quick "shower." I assured him that's about as clean as the pros get. Dave crawled inside the car onto the passenger seat and pulled on warm sweat pants and a long-sleeve rugby shirt. Dave is not a baseball cap guy, but he pulled one down over his slightly matted hair anyway. When he was dressed, Dave leaned back into the seat and stretched both legs out the door and grinned. And asked if Marc had brought any beer.

Marc grunted and tossed him instead a water bottle foaming with recovery drink and returned to cleaning and wiping down the bike. Just a few squeezes of lube here and there, and then he lifted it up onto the roof and clipped it onto the rack. Dave was very ambivalent about the roof rack. He certainly didn't want any scratches to the roof of his car as the bike was clipped in and out. He didn't even want to think of the small scratches from the key chain as Marc locked the barrel bolt, which secured the bike from theft. And he just kept a watchful eye on Marc, who was trying his best not to deserve the supervision.

I drove back to the beach house slowly. Dave sat in front and sipped from his water bottle. Marc was stuck in the back with Dave's dirty clothes.

While Dave was taking a real shower, Marc carried his bike inside the house and leaned it against the wallpaper in the hallway. I sat down at the kitchen table out of breath from carrying all the bags. It's a lot of work supporting a bike rider. I don't usually get this level of treatment, unless it's an official race weekend and the Luna Team's soigneur is on hand to attend to our every need. This is a special deal, one time only for Dave. Marc had already set up his massage table in the living room, so while waiting for Dave to come down for his rub, he tossed a couple of towels into the clothes dryer to warm them up. A few minutes later, Dave descended the stairs and flopped on the table as though it were something he naturally did every day. Marc draped his reclining figure with the warm towels and went to work on his legs.

Dave was getting this pampered treatment today, because 2 days in a row he had put in great rides. The right kind of riding. Dave said he felt great, the last 10 minutes or so at zone 2 feeling as strong as the first. The cooldown had helped, as would the massage. And so would tomorrow's ride. He would be riding tomorrow with low intensity for 2 to 3 hours.

In Dave's case, because he had been estimating his intensity levels, when he thought he was working hard at zone 4 or 5, he really wasn't. It requires some skill to take your own pulse while riding a bike at 20 miles an hour. Guesstimating your intensity zones can be wildly off the mark. Similarly, when Dave thought he was riding easy, at a warmup or recovery pace or zone 1, he was actually going too hard. So in essence, all his rides had been in his zone 3, and that's why his 50-miler had really worked him over. Tomorrow he would again wear the HR monitor and would stay within zone 2. These couple of days on the Eastern Shore, hopefully, would be enough to get Dave back on track with his training plan for a Century Ride.

I've been using a heart monitor for years. When I first bought one, I actually did sleep with it for a week or so. It turned out that in the morning while still lying in bed, taking my own pulse for 15 seconds and then multiplying by 4 was as accurate as reading my HR monitor. So a monitor isn't necessary to determine a resting heart rate. Doctors and nurses simply take a pulse for a few seconds and then do some math. Over the years of diligently training with a monitor, I have also been able to recognize my intensity zones with a fair degree of accuracy. That's just the result of thousands of hours of riding while glancing at the monitor wondering, "How much will this little climb raise my heart rate?" You play games with it. Just like you did when you first got your cycling computer and you tried to keep your cadence as steady as possible at 110 revolutions a minute, or your speed at 17 mph. Training with a monitor does give you a biofeedback loop that enables you to recognize your intensity. I still prefer to use one while training and racing, because sometimes you can get excited by the competition and lose track. But if I've forgotten my heart rate monitor or if the battery dies out, I'm confident that I can usually ride at my desired intensity zones.

Dave's Training Log—
Week 10

Date	Sleep/Wt.	Workout	Notes
Mon	7 hrs/166	1 hr	Easy recovery ride at home
Tue	8 hrs/167		
Wed	8 hrs/167		
Thu	7 hrs/168	2 hrs: 35 miles at beach	Completely flat! Marla and Marc supported; felt pretty good; easy to mod pace
Fri	7 hrs/167	2 hrs: Another good, but flat, ride	Easy pace with tailwind
Sat	8 hrs/168		
Sun	8 hrs/168	1.5 hrs: Last day at beach	Rode at moderate pace, but legs tired

Total Riding Hours: **6.5 hrs!**
Total Miles: **141**

Marla's Training Log— Week 10

Date	Sleep/HR/Wt.	Workout	Notes
Mon	9 hrs/47/140	2 hrs: zones 1–2	Spin with Dave
Tue	9 hrs/43/139	30 min run: zone 2	Easy jog
Wed	9 hrs/46/139	1 hr: zone 2	Easy, flat ride
		2 hrs: zone 3	Trail digging
Thu	6 hrs/46/140	1 hr: zone 2	Easy ride
Fri	8 hrs/45/140	3.5 hrs: zone 2; big group ride	Easy pace, pretty relaxing
Sat	6 hrs/49/139	3 hrs: zone 2	Good mtb ride; technical terrain
Sun	7 hrs/50/140	2.5 hrs: zones 3–4	Nice, hilly ride w/ Dave and group

Total Hours: **15.5**

DAY 71 THROUGH 77 . . .
PAIN HURTS IN A
GOOD WAY

CHAPTER
11

After the big rides on the Eastern Shore last week, I knew Dave would be fatigued. I also knew he wouldn't make a big deal out of it. A high tolerance for pain is a Streb family trait. I myself was still riding my way through the recovery from overtraining, so I was relieved when I swung by Dave's house to see him mowing the lawn. He couldn't be that tuckered out.

Dave's lawn looks too good to putt on. The grass is so green that you want to pour some dressing on it and eat it. The leafy, knotted oak out front spreads a deep shadow in pleasing proportions over the sweeping expanse of grass so that the color shifts from bright pulsing neon to a dark hunter green. As the shadow moves throughout the day, different parts of the lawn look like they're napping. The lawn sweeps around the house, flowing past sharp-edged beds of mulch and flowering bushes to the backyard, where it stops hard against a thicket of green hedge.

It was his off day. Pushing the gas-powered mower was a great activity for him to be engaged in. Enough exertion to break a sweat, but not too much. Mowing worked his arms and shoulders mainly, muscle groups that his riding neglected. The walking part was a good way to keep the blood flowing through his sore leg muscles. But as I coasted down his driveway, I couldn't help but notice that Dave's leggy gait was off-kilter.

Dave is tall and narrow at the hips. Pushing the mower naturally would alter his stride, but his legs seemed stiff and straight. He wasn't bending at the knees. He was marching across the grass in a vaguely Eastern European military fashion. But the falls of his green-stained Adidas were with a certain incongruous delicateness. On his face was a subtle wince with every other step. His beige Dockers didn't seem as Friday casual as usual.

"You're not cutting straight rows!" I joked as I approached him. He spun around and the mower sputtered to a quit.

"Oh! Hey, Marla."

"Right back there. You started swerving."

"I know," he agreed, shaking his head low from side to side with exaggeration.

"Some of the neighbors are gathered down the street," I continued. "There were loud voices and gestures toward your lawn."

A crack of a smile raised his face, and Dave brushed a few grass clippings from his shoulder with the back of his hand.

"And some of them were holding pitchforks and torches. I think they're coming after you, 'cause your lawn is bringing down their property values."

He teased me as we walked around the side of the house about the status of my garden at my row house in the city. That garden amounts to two wooden barrels on the sidewalk out front, each planted with a skeletal bush that budded daily with the fruit of potato chip bags, Pepsi cans, and beer bottle caps. He was right on target.

So I changed the subject.

"You're walking funny. What's the matter?"

He eased himself into the good Adirondack chair and muttered, "Saddle sores." His training had ramped up, both in intensity and in mileage, and his body was beginning to take notice. He maintained a good sense of humor, joking that if there's no pain and therefore no gain, then he must be way ahead of everybody else. Our family trait of having a high tolerance for pain is not necessarily a good thing.

Out of sympathy for his plight, I chose to stand.

Cycling is generally accepted as one of the safest sports per hour of engagement. There are inherent dangers of course, like broken collarbones, road rash, and yes, the more common saddle sores. Saddle problems come in a few different styles. Tingly or "dead" spots "down there" in extreme and rare cases may lead to temporary impotence. I was standing on more firm ground as far as knowing about the most common type of saddle problem: saddle sores.

I let out a deep breath of relief about not having to discuss in depth the possibility of my brother's erectile dysfunction. But still, I didn't really know where to begin talking about saddle sores.

There is the basic chafing right through the spandex of the shorts from the inner thigh rubbing up against the horn of the saddle itself. This can be painful. The inflamed skin can be rubbed so raw that it may result in ulceration. But there is no real reason to let it get to that point. Shorts that have a seam in this area can be the cause. Or the shape of the saddle may be too pronounced. A good skin cream with a topical steroid component can usually clear this up in a few days. And then you should try some new chamois cream or shorts.

Sometimes the sweating and skin irritation may block up some of the sweat glands in this area, and an infection may develop. A lot of bacteria can find its way into a pair of chamois after 3 hours in the saddle, and some of this bacteria can cause you problems, especially if trapped in blocked sweat glands or in contact with areas rubbed raw from chafing. If this is the case, antibacterial creams may be necessary to clear up the situation. If this doesn't work, you may have to consult a doctor. Keeping the skin clean and dry helps. Riding in a fresh pair of shorts helps even more. And well-padded shorts do not mean the *most* padded shorts. You should shop around until you find a pair whose padding thickness, size, and shape suits you the best.

But what was I going to tell Dave about his saddle sores?

He looked up at me with those eyes—the very eyes that my schoolgirl friends had gushed to me were so cute. His eyes were telling me that he was in serious pain and that he was embarrassed. He had no one else to turn to. Lorena would remind him it was his own fault, and deserved, for disappearing down the beach for a couple days last week while she was stuck with the kids and swamped at work. Chris would just mock him about the injury near his manhood. Dave's eyes were pleading. I was all he had left. And I had gotten him into this.

"Get some Brave Soldier salve and rub it on. I'd also use a huge dollop of Bag Balm for every ride."

I quickly spun on my heels in retreat. I didn't think I needed to get into great detail about this with my brother.

From the edge of the deck, I bellowed over my shoulder, "If it looks really bad, go online and do a Google search for pudendal neuropathy."

As I rode away, I really had to concentrate not to go too fast. I was still trying to ride with recovery from overtraining in mind. That made it harder to escape the conclusion that I was a bad sister.

The best way to treat the usual saddle sores is to prevent them in the first place by riding on the right saddle and by riding in the right shorts. In both cases, the right equipment is the equipment that fits best. Treat your equipment well by making sure that both these items are clean and dry. If sores develop, try to bathe as soon as possible after your rides, even if that cuts into your postride latte ritual. If sores persist, you can try Bag Balm, which is available in most drugstores. Just read the instructions on the packaging and don't worry that Bag Balm is formulated for cow udders. And keep in mind that Brave Soldier is intended for civilian applications as well. There are other treatment modalities for saddle sores, but I have no personal knowledge of the Eastern practice of acupuncture or of the traditional European method of stuffing a raw steak down the back of your shorts.

As it turned out, Brave Soldier did the trick. Applying a dab or two to the affected area over the next few days cleared it all up for Dave. He didn't even miss a day of riding. His experience with injury was fairly typical. Cycling is relatively injury-free, but there are a few things to watch out for. Aside from those that result from the trauma of a crash, almost all other injuries occur from overuse and are fairly minor. These overuse injuries can be treated in most cases by a few days' rest, some ice, and elevation. Long-term success can be found with a small equipment change or adjustment to the riding position. A solution can often be found in recognizing one's own capabilities and training so that threshold is not injuriously exceeded.

The myth that there is no pain without gain has ruined many an athletic career. The kernel of truth that lies at the heart of that adage is that during intense exercise, our sensory system registers the by-products released during muscular contraction as pain. So during and after a hard workout, you might experience some muscle soreness. Jane Fonda in her workout videos made this type of pain universally known as the burn. This type of pain is a healthy sign of a good workout. Depending on your level of fitness and which part of your periodized plan you're in, you may have lingering pain. This usually lasts only a day or two.

If lingering pain persists more than 3 days, it may be a sign of overuse. That tells you to back down a notch.

However, if a soreness doesn't develop until 24 to 36 hours after training, like a whiplash comes on a few days after a car accident, it's called delayed-onset muscle soreness (DOMS). It's brought on by the prolonged overuse of the muscles, causing rampant microtears and strains in the individual muscle fibers themselves. Muscles can only contract. When asked to make a full contraction repeatedly over long stretches of time, these individual muscle fibers become worn and torn. In the days following the exercise, each fiber swells with lymph; blood, bringing in fresh oxygen and nutrients; and hormones like cortisol, prolactin, and HGH. These fluids also carry away cellular material by means of phagocytic neutrophils and white blood cells. Repairs to the individual muscle fibers take place on a cellular level. The fibers grow thicker wherever repairs are made. The nerves of the sensory system, however, can only report to the brain that all this activity is going on by firing, "pain, ouch, pain," whenever the muscle contracts during this process.

DOMS can be mitigated and the whole process expedited by an easy spin, stretching, and massage.

The body is highly adaptable to stress loads. That's how muscles develop. If you subject the body to an excessive training load and do not allow the body enough time to adapt to that load, it will cause injury, and you'll feel its pain. The bottom line is that you cannot train efficiently while repairs to the muscles are ongoing. Repairing injuries to tendons, joints, and skins might take even longer.

Here's the list of usual suspects of pain caused by overuse.

1. Improper training

   - Too many miles too soon

   - Too much hill intensity

   - Too big a gear

   - Improper recovery

2. Poor body position on the bike, resulting in knee, back, neck, or hand pain

   - Sitting too far fore or aft

   - Improper stem length or rise

   - Improper bar width

   - Improper crank length or pedal position

3. Inherent physiology

   - Excessively misaligned foot or hand bones

   - Leg length differences causing knee, hip, and back pain

• Knock-knees causing anterior knee pain

• A preexisting condition, such as an old football injury, that may not make itself apparent until you start training for a Century Ride

Saddle Sores

If during the first few weeks you progressively increase the load of your training, you stand a chance of not experiencing any pain at all—not even from your butt. What happens is as you become fitter and stronger, as your muscles adapt to the workload, the nerves and skin and blood vessels in your shorts adapt as well.

The nerves in the affected area of your shorts can become irritated, but after riding steadily for weeks in a row, they'll adapt. They simply become used to the prospect that you will be spending some time in the saddle. They'll fire less often and less intensely, especially as the dermal and epidermal skin layers in the area thicken and callous as one would expect. Just as one can develop a gardener's green thumb, thickly callused and impenetrable to thorns, so too will you develop a bicyclist's butt.

I know it doesn't sound too great, but it does work out well in the end.

PREVENTION OF SADDLE SORES

1. Make sure your saddle fits. Time will tell. Keep in mind width, curvature, padding, and horn.

2. Try changing the tilt of your saddle.

3. Hygiene is huge. I know this may sound obvious, but always riding in clean shorts is a really good idea. Washing with an antibacterial soap before and after riding helps.

4. Products like Brave Soldier, Chamois Butt'r, Bag Balm, and other lubricants can reduce friction, sweating, and bacteria.

TREATMENT OF SADDLE SORES

1. If the sore is the size of a pimple, wash with antibacterial soap and apply salve three times daily. Leave the sore unbandaged.

2. If the sore has grown in appearance and size to a boil, then it needs to come to a head to drain. Three hot baths daily increase blood-flow to the area and enhance the body's own immune system.

3. You may need to apply a drawing salve and cover the sore with a bandage. The combination of pressure on the boil while riding and the effect of a drawing salve like Boil Ease speeds up the process.

Usually saddle sores are not so painful or injurious in themselves that you cannot ride while they heal. Along with all the creams out there, a couple of Advil can do no harm. But in rare cases, if your saddle sores don't respond to these treatments after a few days, then you should consider medical help. Prescription antibiotics and steroids may be required. In all my years of riding and racing bikes, I have never had a saddle sore a little salve couldn't fix.

Women's Issues

Women have very few special considerations, unless of course they're pregnant. In that case, back off the training slightly, avoid overhreating, and don't crash! There haven't been any studies showing that women's menstrual cycles affect their performance negatively, unless they're prone to severe cramping. Women can ride as long as men, and at the same relative intensities. We may be more picky about our saddles, and luckily there are many on the market addressing our feminine anatomies.

Knee Pain

A common knee pain is in the patellar, or kneecap, area. The bottom part of this region can become quite tender while riding and even more so afterward when the natural masking agents of adrenaline and endorphins wear off. This pain is most typically caused by a sudden jump in mileage or hill climbing, or mashing, which is using too big a gear for long periods. The patella becomes "overused" as the kneecap struggles to slide and glide over the gap between thigh and shin bones while the rider exerts too great a force by cranking away.

The adjustment is pretty straightforward. Reduce your mileage until your body has recovered, and then only increase your mileage in manageable loads. A weekly total increase in mileage that seems to work well for most is 10 percent. This is called progressive load training. I prefer to gauge work levels in time and the use of intensity zones rather than mileage, because road conditions vary so much. Changing your riding style from a mashing low rpm to a higher spinning rpm can greatly relieve the forces on your knees.

If an adjustment to your training doesn't provide pain relief, then it's time to address your equipment. Patellar knee pain is also often caused by riding with your saddle too low. Your cranks may be too long, or your bottom bracket too wide. Even though you might have been fitted for your bike at a reputable shop, you'll be surprised at how just a few millimeters difference in pedal float can affect your knee. It may be worth going back to the shop to have those millimeters adjusted.

Other problems with knees are:

1. **Posterior:** Pain at the back of the knee is caused by swelling of the biceps femoris, which is the tendon that anchors the lower part of the hamstring to the top of the fibular shinbone. It's from too high a saddle, mashing big gears, or poor flexibility of the hamstring muscles.

2. **Medial:** Pain on the inside of the knee is often the result of inflammation of the anserine tendon or bursa. Some causes are foot pronation, riding with bowlegs or knock-knees, or even exiting from some clipless pedal systems.

3. **Lateral:** Outside knee pain is often associated with inflammation of the iliotibial tendon/bursa. Iliotibial band syndrome affects women more frequently than men because of women's wider hips. It also can be caused by too low a saddle, too narrow a bottom bracket, or a pointed-inward foot position.

I have one leg slightly longer than the other. I didn't find out until relatively recently when my Luna Women's Mountain Bike Team's soigneur, Waldek Stepniowski, first got me on his massage table. I have always experienced lower-back pain during the early spring when I'm training the heaviest. For years, I thought that was the price of being a pro, and all I could do was learn to live with it and hope for a good massage now and then to relieve some of the pain. Wally worked on my lower back for a minute or two and then he flipped me over on his "table of truth," as we riders refer to his massage table, so that I was lying on my back. He lifted both my heels and vigorously shook my legs like they were mariachis. He then laid them down side by side, ankle next to ankle. But not quite. My right ankle bone didn't evenly line up with my left. My right leg was just a little longer than my left.

I was shocked. As an athlete, I thought I knew my body. Even more disturbing was the revelation that my original equipment was faulty. Wally told me to relax. It wasn't a big deal. Leg length disparities are very common and easily dealt with. When you get fitted for your bike, the saddle height, frame size, and crank length are usually all determined assuming the rider has two legs of equal length. So, sometimes both legs don't actually get measured.

Wally suggested I place an orthotic insert in my shoe on my shorter leg. He said I should try a shim only half as thick as the difference in my leg lengths. Just that much of a correction should help lessen my back pain. If I wanted, he said over time I could gradually increase the thickness of the shim to the exact size, but I never bothered. That half-thickness shim eliminated almost 90 percent of my back pain. The difference between my leg lengths isn't so great that I wear shoe implants off the bike in my running and casual shoes, but that's an adjustment to consider.

Hand, Neck, and Back Pain

For most types of pain, there are simplistic anagrams like RICE: Rest, Ice, Compress, and Elevate. But the diagnosis and treatment of painful conditions should be sought from a qualified sports physician. At the Stone Clinic in San Francisco, I have had my knees successfully scoped, a posterior cruciate ligament (PCL) rebuilt with a cadaver's ligament, an anterior cruciate ligament (ACL) reattached, and the meniscus trimmed to repair motocross injuries. The bones in my thumb were voluntarily fused together at The Hand Clinic in San Francisco. A section of my clavicle was removed at The Scripps Research Institute in La Jolla, California, as a surgical solution to repeatedly breaking my collarbone when I was first learning to jump mountain bikes. RICE can only help so much. With that in mind, other common painful conditions that can arise affecting major body parts are listed below.

1. Hand pain is usually caused by the compression of two nerves, the ulnar and median nerves, and by the overuse of the tendons of the thumb. Treatment for these conditions is affecting a consciously lighter grip. A light grip works best, but thicker bar tape or better-padded gloves can also help. Frequent changing of the hand position from the hoods to the drops to the center helps, too.

2. Neck and back pain are nearly universal at times whether you're training on a bike or not. Neck pain is usually caused by the strain of holding the weight of your head upright. Back pain is usually the result of the compression of the lower back from prolonged standing or sitting (as when on a bicycle). The best treatment is simply to ride through any pain if it's not too severe, as it usually disappears as mysteriously as it develops without any

long-term implications. For neck pain, try to move your head frequently as you ride. Stretch your neck up and down and side to side. Secondarily, consider increasing the rise of your stem, or decreasing its length. Raise your bar or try a more shallow drop. Sometimes a frame with a shorter top tube is necessary. To relieve lower-back pain, move for and aft on the saddle frequently, stand on your pedals, and stretch your back during descents. Oftentimes lower-back pain is the result of a lack of core strength in the abdominals. Situps and crunches can fix that.

It's always easier to advocate prevention rather than treatment for any of the above painful conditions. The prevention of the conditions that give rise to these types of pain is usually to be found in laying a good foundation on which to build your training base, and then during the heavy training part of your periodization limiting yourself to weekly total increases of less than 10 percent. Remember, after building for 3 weeks, take 1 week easier for recovery.

Managing the Healthy Pain

Most cyclists experience a more "healthy" pain. The first part of this chapter was a worst-case scenario for pain. All in all, cycling is an injury-free sport when compared to jogging, skiing, and surfing. With merely some very commonsense precautions, riding a hundred miles can be enjoyed pain- and injury-free by nearly everybody.

Not all pain is bad. Pain doesn't always signal that the body has been injured. Most of the time the sensation of pain merely indicates that the body is adapting. Brushing up against your performance threshold followed by an appropriate recovery is the simplest and most effective way to increase your training base and riding fitness. But where is that commonsense threshold, the point where it hurts so much there's no way it can be any good for you? Where is the point where you can recognize that pain is still a good thing, a healthy sign of exertion, and then what do you do with that knowledge?

Unfortunately, there is no a priori recognition of the point where pain ceases to be a good thing. As a society, we have ordered our lives so that every incidence of pain is an opportunity for intervention. The moment a tingle of pain evidences itself, we react to eliminate it.

All too often, we respond to a pang of hunger, no matter how slight, by eating. And look where that has gotten us as a society. In Japan, it is a cultural norm to cease eating a meal while still a tiny bit hungry. It's polite to leave about 20 percent of the meal on the plate. Here, we sometimes eat until it almost hurts, and then we have to sleep it off afterward. We have forgotten that the weak rumble of a midafternoon hunger pang is simply a by-product of digestion from food that was eaten at lunch. That little flutter doesn't mean you should speed-dial for pizza to be delivered in 30 minutes or less.

The proof is that if you simply wait a few minutes; the hunger pang will disappear; that part of the digestive process will have ceased. And it turns out that you were never really hungry after all. There never was any real need to order that pizza.

We react similarly when engaged in the normal habit of walking. The moment we experience a feeling, or sensation, we interpret that as pain, and we immediately react to prevent further pain: We stop walking. If we had just continued on for a distance, we might have discovered that the walking sensation wasn't pain, just like that sensation of digesting was not a hunger pang, but rather each was a normal, healthy sensory signal that our bodies were merely reacting to stimuli.

A lot of Americans, even young healthy ones, don't walk up stairs. They prefer escalators or elevators. The sensation of one's own weight felt in the quadriceps, hamstrings, and calves as one walks up a flight of stairs has come to be interpreted as a kind of pain. A walk along a beach, or a hike through a flowery field, "hurts." We've become so divorced from what the normal, healthy feeling of moving our bodies through this world should be that we choose not to.

We arrange our lives so that we don't have to move our bodies. If you live in a neighborhood where there are no sidewalks, just roads for cars, what other conclusion can you come to, other than you shouldn't be walking? You become used to the habit of not walking very much at all. On the day after Thanksgiving, when the parking lot at the mall is filled up and the only spot you can find to park is many rows from the mall entrance, the strange and unfamiliar feeling in your legs as you carry your own weight across a distance of a few hundred feet can only be interpreted as pain. And pain is to be avoided; we still know that much. That's why you vow to get to the mall earlier in the morning next year for the big shopping day after Thanksgiving, so you won't have to endure the "pain" of walking across a parking lot.

Unfortunately, we live in a society where the simple act of walking has become so rare that high-tech alternatives to it have become legally recognized. The federal government has passed a law that recognizes anybody riding on a human transporter as a legal pedestrian. Legally, a person riding on a human transporter is the same as a person who is walking. I guess the unicycle lobby isn't as powerful as the human transporter industry, because a unicyclist is still not a legal pedestrian.

It's no wonder then that walking for 5 or 6 hours throughout the course of the day has become almost unheard of. Rarer still is riding a bike. Cycling is more energy efficient than walking, and therefore easier (okay, on flats). Yet when you tell friends that you plan to ride your bike for 5 to 7 hours, the average duration of a Century Ride, they think you're nuts. That you must be an extreme athlete! So few people walk or ride a bike for a few hours at a time nowadays that we have forgotten what it feels like when we do! That legs will tingle, breathing will become deeper, and there is a chance of perspiration. But the next day, there will be no evidence of injury, so therefore those sensations in the legs and lungs while riding a bike for 5 or 6 hours the day before were not pain. They were simply the feeling of riding a bike.

Keep in mind that in most cases while you're on the bike, what you're experiencing is not pain at all, but rather the normal feelings of exertion. These feelings, which may seem strange and frightening at first, can grow on you. Just as the first sip of lite beer might not have tasted so great during that first frat party your freshman year of college, but 7 years later at your graduation party you have developed an appreciation for a fine amber ale, so too can you learn to appreciate those bike riding feelings. These feelings are caused by adrenaline and endorphins, which are released into the bloodstream during exertion. This sensation is more commonly known as runner's high, or being in the zone. It, too, is completely normal and beneficial. It's during this part of the ride, even though you might be under great exertion, that you actually relax and bask in the bath of endorphins that your body is producing for you. This is the part of physical exercise that is the great stress reducer that everybody always talks about.

How can getting up earlier than normal before work, squeezing into formfitting clothes, putting on a goofy helmet, and going for a bike ride reduce stress? Just ask anyone who has. They will tell you. The perceived pain during their first rides has become transformed into a pleasure. After 30 or 45 minutes of riding, heart pumping, legs working, lungs ballooning, none of this painful, but all of it wonderfully sensational, they're riding in the zone. This is what reduces the stress levels.

You may feel this glow for a few hours after riding. If you're riding your bike regularly, rather than feeling tired afterward, it's more likely that you'll feel more energetic. Don't be surprised if rather than taking the elevator, you now decide to walk up a flight of stairs. Even if you have already ridden that morning and it may seem therefore more logical that you would be tired. But what happens is that you have grown to associate the sensation and feeling of your leg muscles contracting and flexing with something pleasurable. So in order to enjoy the pleasure, you seek out ways to make your muscles contract.

Suddenly, it all makes sense, doesn't it?

If I have enjoyed a particularly good workout that day, after dinner, when I should be exhausted, there is nothing I enjoy more than going for a brief walk around the neighborhood. Each step of the way my legs tingle with a delicate soreness, a soft caress of heightened awareness, because my circulatory system is still flooded with the endorphins from that day's ride. Each step pumps the blood, giving me another quick hit. It's very relaxing, even if I find myself strolling through the dark and narrow alleyways of Fells Point in Baltimore's oldest neighborhood. If I didn't ride that day, my after-dinner stroll is not as rewarding, because there are no endorphins in my system. If I haven't ridden in a couple of days, my evening walk is downright frustrating. But that's just me.

So even though there may be a few occasions where real pain is associated with cycling, if you make sure your bike fits and you don't crash, what you think is pain is actually a wonderful feeling that you simply aren't familiar with. At first, use your training log to help make the distinction. If you're out with your group ride and the paceline is heating up too quickly for you, sit in through a couple of rotations until you feel you have recovered enough to pull without causing a case of DOMS for yourself. Don't necessarily quit riding for the day just because the group is too fast for you. Keep pedaling, and you will be surprised how easily the pain transcends into pleasure.

Dave's Training Log— Week 11

Date	Sleep/Wt.	Workout	Notes
Mon	9 hrs/166		
Tue	8 hrs/167		(raked some leaves)
Wed	8 hrs/167	1 hr: easy spin	Too tired to go harder, saddle sores were distracting
Thu	10 hrs/168		
Fri	9 hrs/169		
Sat	8 hrs/168	1 hr: rode hard up climbs	Feeling better—saddle sores finally healed up; legs completely recovered
Sun	8 hrs/168		

Total Riding Hours: **2**
Total Miles: **35**

Marla's Training Log— Week 11

Date	Sleep/HR/Wt.	Workout	Notes
Mon	9 hrs/47/140	2 hrs: zones 1–2	
Tue	9 hrs/43/140	1.5 hrs: zones 3–4 hill repeats 5x5 min efforts	Felt great; stopped by Dave's
Wed	9 hrs/46/139	1 hr: zone 2 2 hrs: zone 3	Easy, flat ride Strenuous trail digging
Thu	6 hrs/46/140	1 hr: zone 2	Easy ride
Fri	8 hrs/45/140	3.5 hrs: zones 2–4	Big group ride Lots of energy; rode well
Sat	6 hrs/49/139	3 hrs: zone 2	Good mtb ride, technical terrain
Sun	7 hrs/50/140	2.5 hrs: zones 3–4	Nice, hilly ride

Total Hours: **16.5**

DAY 78 THROUGH 84 . . .
FINE POINTS

CHAPTER
12

Dave and I are rolling through the hills near Frederick. I'm having a lot of fun. I think Dave is, too, but I can't tell because he's breathing so hard. The road just rises and falls over the terrain like the wrinkles in a blanket thrown across a bed. It doesn't really seem like climbing, because you don't really have time to establish that regular, painful, deep-breathing rhythm. But the small hills sneak up on you nonetheless. These are the kind that are just big enough that you can't just stand and stamp your pedals right over them. You just have to deal with them. Or find a way to enjoy them.

Dave hasn't quite figured this out yet. He starts strong at the bottom of every hill. Too strong. Like he's pretending that the slope beneath his wheels is a mirage. For a while, he can stay on top of his gear, but then he starts to lose his cadence.

I have a great view of this drama from just a few feet behind him.

Taking advantage of the draft

As long as he's carrying all that speed, I might as well draft off him and enjoy the show.

About a third of the way up most of these little 2-minute hills, Dave figures out that he has to shift into an easier gear. But I guess he's not as swift with his Ergo levers as he is with his power mouse, because he always shifts just a tad late. The strain on his chain makes its movement onto the cog a struggle. Dave breaks his cadence. Nothing big to the casual eye, only to another cyclist on the hill watching your every move. Dave breaks his pedal stroke for a second, and during that pause the loud click and clang of his shifting sounds down the street. I can see his hips hung up, frozen for a second as he waits for the chain to drop onto the cog's teeth—downshifting without a clutch. Before Dave has any chance of realizing that he can never make the jump with me, I scoot around him on up the hill.

Behind me I can hear him breathing even harder. Then I can hear a fistful of finger shifting and some cursing.

I stay just far enough away to let him know who's boss, and then I start to swing lazily across the road over the center line from shoulder

David Smith

Hitting the descent

to shoulder. When a hill is really steep and you're already in your granny gear, sometimes that's the only way that you can make the grade, by cutting a less steep path across its face. But I'm just doing it to annoy my big brother.

The top of the hill is in sight. Dave has pulled even with me. His gear is way too big. I know he wants to ease up. I know he wants to believe that we're there. I can tell by how hard he's wracking his bar from side to side. But I don't let him ease up. I feel great. Enjoying the little rest I had while I was waiting for him. But now that he's here, almost at the top, it's time for some cat-and-mouse play. I wait until the moment I see his shoulders relax, when his arms stop wrestling with his bar. That means he's done working; he's at the top.

I click and then I'm gone again. The top is a good 50 feet long. And slightly up, still. Might as well be a mile. Funny how the mind really wants to deny the curvature of the earth. We always think we're at the top when we obviously are not. Dave hasn't recognized this exercise-induced illusion as a common cycling trap. I love springing this trap. You have to be sneaky like that when you're not a very strong climber.

I pedal hard right over and through the transition at the top. By the time Dave gets to where he can see me descending, I am a blurry, tucking bullet. Because I'm finished being cruel, down at the bottom I take a sip of water. Wipe my glasses a few times until he catches up.

Afterward, I'll buy the beer. It's the least I can do.

There is a lot of talk in our sport about technology, but not technique. Probably because it's more fun for a consumer to flip through a new parts catalog with all the latest carbon fiber, titanium, and NASA techno mumbo jumbo. I admit that I really find myself staring at the glossy color charts comparing strength-to-weight ratios of various manufacturers' bars, stems, and cranks. I wonder how the weight savings in a new carbon fiber frame affects its modulus? At the trade shows, I try to squeeze truth from the new crop of tire rubber: How much does the higher durometer reading affect its rolling resistance? I'm a bike geek, after all.

The marketing departments of the bike industry have already figured out that it's hard enough to move units that are new and improved, lighter and stronger, more value per dollar. Imagine how hard it would be to meet their sales projections if they just told you to ride better. You don't have to get all the new stuff. The secret of how has to do with technique, not technology.

Riding a bike is simple; that's one of its great virtues. But simple things are often more complicated than we realize. Ever try to figure out which is better for the environment, using a plastic bag or a paper bag for your groceries? It's the same with riding a bike. Climbing up a hill and then coming down a hill—but, as Jack and Jill could tell you, even something as simple as that is not without its problems. When do you use your brakes? That seems like an obvious one, doesn't it? How do you corner? Easy. But not really.

Climbing

Climbing holds a disproportionate place in the pantheon of cycling's various specialties. Admit it. At the coffee shop after a road ride, rarely are there comments that someone else is really great at cornering. You never hear, "Boy, that guy really knows line selection." It would seem downright silly to praise a riding buddy for his tucking prowess.

Okay, credit is given appropriately to time trialers. But when was the last time you heard accolades for a roadie's descending ability? Climbing gets the lion's share of our respect and admiration. It's true, more time can be gained up a mile-long climb than down a mile-long descent. Just like blondes have more fun, it's not a question of fairness, just an admission of reality.

Most of that reality is that good climbing often separates good riders from all the rest. I am sure you have been on rides where you have hung in there, taken your pulls, stayed at the front . . . until that one hill where you fell off the back. During a 2-hour ride, you just didn't have it during that 10-minute climb, so by the time you made it to the fruit stand, everybody else in the group had nearly finished their smoothies.

The climb was only 10 minutes, so how did your ride fall apart? Once the group left you behind and made it to the top, they were able to work together to fight the air's resistance, not just during the descent but for the rest of the day. You blew up on the hill, and it took the whole descent and a good part of the flat afterward to recover. You were left to struggle on alone. Maybe your spirit was tamped down just a bit, too.

The ability to climb well is rewarded disproportionately. It seems a little unfair.

In the context of hill repeats, your climbing technique wasn't as important as your repeats. Your hill repeats by design are supposed to end in ragged, messy style. You are supposed to ride to your failure point during a hill repeat, and then take as much time as you need to recover before doing another. Any way that you can make it up the hill 10 times during an hour's ride is going to be beneficial.

But now that you're a stronger rider, there are some subtleties that may help to make you a better climber on the big hills. During a group ride, at the top of a hill climb, you might want to be able to continue with the group on your attack. You want to finish a hill climb strong and power over the crest.

1. With momentum from the previous downhill or flat, start out at the bottom of the hill in a moderate gear, or about 90 rpm. As you get into the climb, shift one or two gears at a time, and shift slightly before you really need to. A misshift or a dropped chain can really ruin your cadence and momentum. Shifting early while taking a lighter pedal stroke is much easier on the drivetrain.

2. Unless you're Lance, you shouldn't go completely anaerobic on a climb. If you have been riding with a heart monitor and riding within your target intensity zones, then it should be no big deal to climb just under your anaerobic threshold. Usually standing raises the heart rate a few beats per minute. You want to keep that in mind if you're near your limit.

3. If you're trying to become a better climber, you can exceed your anaerobic threshold for a short time. And then recover. And then exceed it again. And recover. Lather hard, rinse easy, repeat. Progressively increasing the duration and intensity at which you exceed your threshold is a quick way to become a stronger climber.

4. On a big hill, sitting is the best way to stay aerobic and make sure you get to the top without blowing up. Occasionally standing is a good way to give certain muscles a break, but it does use up about 30 percent more energy. On short, rolling hills, it's okay to stand when you feel comfortable that the top is within your threshold. This gives you more momentum for the flat. On short, steep hills, stand early in the transition and jam on your pedals up the hill. This is the best way to maintain your speed over the top.

5. When you're standing, allow the bike to sway a bit from side to side. This gives your arms better leverage, and power to the

pedals increases. But don't allow this motion to become exaggerated, because any energy expended on moving sideways will not get you up the hill. Let the slight sway become part of your pedaling rhythm and cadence.

6. Out of the saddle, climbing in the right gear should make your leg muscles feel like you're walking up stairs. If your rpm is so low that you're almost in a trackstand at times, then your gear is too big. But, if you feel like your legs are bouncing up and down and you are unable to make smooth circles, then your gear is too small. A good climbing cadence is around 60 to 80 rpm.

7. Triple chainrings are not a bad idea for a Century. If you ride in the Sierras or the Rockies, or even on the daunting hills in your hometown, then you'll find adding a third chainring makes sense. There are steep hills on the East Coast as well, none steeper than Mount Washington. So if you want more gearing, go for it.

8. It is very important to make circles. The up-and-down, piston type of pedaling is inefficient, but even more so on a climb. Try to imagine you're scraping mud off the soles of your shoes at the top and bottom parts of your pedal stroke. This will help you put out power in most of the rotation.

9. Relax your upper body as much as possible. This saves energy for pedaling. I like to keep my hands on the brake hoods for a more upright position. It makes breathing easier. Lightly rest your hands on the hoods or on the bar top. There is no aerodynamic penalty when sitting up, since most climbing speeds are so slow.

10. Slide around on the saddle. Moving forward works your quadriceps and gives your butt and hamstrings a break. Moving aft works your butt and gives your quads a reprieve.

11. If you're racing, power over the top of the crest. Don't stop climbing when you get to the top. Don't even stop climbing

when you're riding across the flat summit of the top. You have to climb right on over, shifting and standing as needed, carrying as much speed as possible right into the descent. That's when you can recover. Failing to do so can negate all of your previous hard work.

Descending

I have more experience downhilling than I do uphilling, that's true. As a two-time mountain bike NORBA National Downhill Champion, a World Cup winner, and an X Games Gold Medalist, I learned a few things about riding a bike down a hill. Part of what I learned is that a good downhiller has to be a powerful and explosive pedaler. There is a misconception that pedaling is not as important as other aspects of downhilling such as cornering, braking points, and line selection. But a good downhiller has to have great fitness and power. Too many people are mistaken when they think that in a downhill race you are mainly coasting.

Honestly, it's almost impossible on a road ride to make up all the time during a descent that was lost on a climb. It's a function of time versus speed. The time on a hill climb and the disparity between differing power outputs are greater factors than the speed disparities attained during the descent, especially because of its shorter duration.

But time is time. And, if you're interested in completing or winning a Century Ride, anywhere you can shave off a minute is worth taking a look at. During rides and races, I've made up more time on descents than most people would even consider. A lot of those riders who were stronger climbers than I, thought going downhill was a time to sit up and coast. As the event progressed, my accumulated recoveries from transition momentum and tucking added up. Toward the end, I had more to draw from. If this is your first Century Ride, a little speed with not much extra effort on those downhills will pay off.

And I'm not saying you should keep on pedaling down the hill like a madman or wicked woman, either. There is such a thing as terminal cycling velocity. There's a point where the disturbance to the airflow as you pedal down the hill exceeds the speed gained by the efforts of your pedaling. At around 35 miles an hour, pedaling ceases to be efficient. Beyond this point, pedaling usually slows you down. This is when an aerodynamic tuck is faster than pedaling.

In a good tuck, a rider should pull his arms and legs toward the torso, decreasing the frontal surface area. The lower you can get, the better. Make sure to stay compact but still relaxed. You'll feel yourself accelerating, and this is when you might start smiling.

Riding a bike at these high speeds is not for the fainthearted. Passing cars while riding a bike going downhill is not something I advocate, but it's something that I do on a regular basis. As a rider, you have to recognize your comfort level. At what speed does it stop being exhilarating and become terrifying? You might want to back off around here and sit up tall. This will slow you down.

Aero Tuck Position

1. Stop pedaling.

2. If any steering is to be done while in the aero tuck, it will not be accomplished by your hands on the bar, but by the *gentle* and steady pressure of your inner thighs against the sides of the horn of your saddle. Simply turn your head toward the exit of the turn.

3. Your pedals should be in the neutral position and carrying the preponderance of your body weight. A high center of gravity is not a good idea during an aero tuck; it could cause instability.

4. No sudden moves.

5. Your knees should also be pointed inward, if possible, gently squeezing your top tube.

6. Lean forward so that your back is flat and your butt is high in the air. Keep a small bend at the knee to absorb road vibration.

7. Your hands should be in the drops, with fingers resting on the brakes. This gives you better leverage in case sudden braking is needed.

8. Your head should be right over your stem. Keeping your chin up, like a cheetah, is very important.

9. Your elbows will be bent tightly along your sides as though they were folded bird wings.

10. To get yourself out of a tuck, simply sit up and feel yourself slow down.

While you're tucking, enjoy the free speed and recovery. It does take some practice to relax when you're rocketing down a hill at 40 or 50 mph, separated from being transformed into a long patch of wet roadkill by a skinny tire inflated to 120 psi and the hope that no squirrels plan on crossing the road any time soon. Take some well-earned deep breaths.

Tucking for more speed

David Smith

As a rider, you should always be looking down the road rather than just at the square patch of ground directly in front of your front wheel. It's easy at times to forget that. Riding with a group or in a paceline makes it easy to rely on others to point out road hazards and course changes. But when you're in a screaming descent, even a paceline descent, as sometimes happens during the pro stages, you have to look down the road, in front of the other riders. There simply isn't much time to react, nor room.

If there is an obstruction down the road, like a dog chasing a cat across the street or a patch of broken glass, you should look for an alternate line and slow down if necessary. Resist grabbing a handful of brake. The last thing in the world the rider behind you expects is for you to come to a skidding, two-wheel-drifting stop right in front of him. By the time you get to where the dog was in the middle of the road, the mutt has already crossed. If the dog has hip dysplasia, lean your bike so that you will gently scribe a course behind Fido.

Looking far down the road also helps you avoid surprises. When you ride with your chin up high in the air and your eyes focused some distance down the road, a whole other sensory system comes into play. It's the autonomic sensory system. This is the primitive sensory system from our evolutionary past, or if you prefer, the sensory system that has biologically changed over time. This is the sensory system that allows us to run through the woods without looking where our feet are going. It's the system that enables us to close our mouths the picosecond before we swallow a bug. It's what enables baseball players to start to swing at a pitch within a fraction of a second after it's thrown at 100 miles an hour and hit the white blur without really thinking about it. This is the sensory system that allows you to ride down the hill at such great speeds without worrying about looking for potholes or deep cracks in the pavement.

If you ride staring at those obstacles, you will see yourself riding right smack into them. Happens all the time to beginning riders. But, if you look far down the road, keeping your chin up and balancing like a monkey does when he's swinging, you'll react autonomically. You will have already seen the pothole, and your body will have made the correct adjustment to avoid it without even being really aware of it.

The ability to rely on this intuitive sense is not only a great asset, but it's easy to develop. Ride along the white line on a solo ride. Try to balance on it while staring down at your front wheel. Then try it while looking far ahead with your chin up. It should be noticeably easier to stay on the line when your head's up. Practice looking ahead at all times, and you'll see marked improvement almost immediately.

Looking down the road is important any time you're riding a bike. But it is crucial when you're descending, and not to do it is suicidal when you're in an aero tuck.

Another important and fun aspect of descending is drafting and slingshotting.

SLINGSHOTTING

First of all, you need a big descent. Let's assume that you're pedaling hard over the top of the hill into the descent. As you do, you might catch the climbers who passed you just before first sight of the hill's crest and slowed down immediately because they thought that they were at the top. They are now resting, as they coast down the hill. After you reach your maximum pedaling speed and get into your tuck, you will notice that you're gaining ground on the guy down the hill in front of you. He's sitting up and sipping from his water bottle without a care in the world—after all, he worked really hard to pass you on the climb, didn't he?

While he's still some distance ahead of you, as much as 20 or 30 feet, if you swing your bike behind him, into his slipstream, you will discover that your speed ramps up quite a bit. His inefficient aerodynamic shape is roiling the air in front of you. The disturbed air he's leaving in his wake creates less friction for you as you pass through it than it had for him as he passed through it when it was undisturbed. The rider in front of you is physically paving the way for you.

Carefully stay in his slipstream, and you will quickly be pulled right up to his rear tire. It will seem as pronounced as if an invisible bungee cord were pulling you right to him. You'll see that if you swing out to either side a bit, you slow down. Duck back behind him, and you speed up. Keep your finger on your rear brake just in case. If you time it right, when you want to pass him, you can build up such a great momentum from his slipstream that you can slingshot right around him. Don't just pass him and then allow him to sit in on your slipstream, unless you have a crush on him. Whip past him and flick him off your tail by staying way off to the side so that you are just a speeding blur in the corner of his peripheral vision.

Sometimes it's faster not to pass when descending. I weigh only 139.9 pounds, and I find that the limiting factor of my body weight prevents me from reaching speeds that are easily attainable from simply sitting in the slipstream of a much heavier guy. I can ride downhill much faster behind a guy who weighs 200 pounds than I can by trying to pass him. Marc weighs 200 pounds, and the moment I slip past him, I notice my relative speed dropping as he invariably speeds past a few moments later. As a matter of fact, it's even faster for the both of us if I ride to within an inch of Marc's rear wheel (as long as he doesn't know it, 'cause he gets scared) than it is if he's riding all by himself. The pressure wave created by the both of us is increased by my added weight, and the wave, as it flows over the top of my helmet and down my flat back, pushes us faster down the hill. This effect is really evident if you watch the Tour de France coverage during the long descents from the Alps. You can actually see a long string of riders, sometimes numbering more than two dozen, easily passing at speeds exceeding 50 miles an hour the small Fiats and Mini Coopers that are supposed to be their escort vehicles.

BRAKING

1. Your front brake has 80 percent of your total braking power. Grabbing too much front brake at once can cause you to go right over the bar. That's called an endo. A fun way to impress teenagers is to modulate an endo so your rear wheel rises off the ground. Okay, so it's not absolutely necessary to learn this trick.

Because the front brake is so much more powerful, it's important to modulate it carefully when slowing. Always relax your arms and shoulders during braking, because this helps handling and control. Move your body weight slightly backward and down during braking. Be sure to keep most of your weight on your pedals. In every situation, a low center of gravity is best.

2. Using your rear brake is safer when riding in a group. Its stopping power is considerably less, and that's why you can't get into too much trouble by overusing it in an emergency stop. You might skid the rear wheel a little, but you won't fly over the handlebar. If you're skidding, you want to release the brake slightly to allow your rear wheel to resume rolling. The rear-wheel drift is closely related to the two-wheel drift, which is also related to *highsiding*, but I won't go there.

3. Disc brakes are much more effective than any of the traditional road-style brakes, either V-brakes, calipers, or center-pulls. First of all, disc brakes have way more stopping power. Secondly, they

Under hard braking

are easier to modulate and get a feel for. Disc brakes work better in the rain than any rim-style brake system since the disc has a smaller surface area to get wet, and the location of the disc close to the hub protects its surface from road grime and dirt, whereas rim brakes have a potentially much larger surface area to be negatively affected by rain, dirt, and grime. An insurmountable problem with rim-based braking systems is the potential damage that road grime and dirt could cause once it becomes imbedded in the brake pads. Disc brakes have recently approached and even surpassed the traditional braking systems in weight savings.

The only drawback to disc brakes is that you can't get them on a road bike. They are excellent on mountain bikes, tandems, and touring bikes. People love them on recumbents and even low riders—just not on road bikes. They were even recently made unavailable on cyclocross bikes.

Why?

Cycling's governing body, the UCI, Union Cycliste Internationale, passed a rule outlawing disc brakes on road bikes for racing. And since most manufacturers find it cost-prohibitive to run two different production lines, one for racing and one for the recreational market, they chose to adhere to the UCI rule. So if you're only interested in riding a few Centuries; don't plan on entering any competitive, sanctioned road races; want disc brakes; and can afford a custom road frame from a small builder, I would get the go-ahead and buy them. Disc brakes are that good.

Cornering

Cornering on a road bike seems pretty basic. But a few tips can help you corner more safely and effectively.

1. Keep your head up at all times. Scope out the apex, which is the middle, of the turn. The greater the arc of the apex, the faster you can enter the turn.

2. Relax your arms, shoulders, and back. This will allow your autonomic nervous system to make subtle adjustments.

3. If you need to slow down, do so well before the turn begins. Be sure to be off the brakes before you enter the corner. Dragging a brake in the turn will cause the bike to stand straight up, possibly running you off the road. Plus, braking will kill your exit speed.

4. Enter the corner from the outside of the lane, arc gently toward the apex at the inside of the legal lane, then drift outside again at the exit. Try to scribe only one arc in a corner.

5. Put 95 percent of your body weight on your outside pedal during the turn. This will keep your tires from sliding and will give you more control. Push slightly forward on the inside handlebar.

The Elements

Rain

Rain is unavoidable. Most of the time it's not a big deal. Either you got caught out in it unprepared during the middle of your ride, or you dressed for rain, slapped on fenders, and once you got out on the road, the clouds broke and the sun peeked through.

If it starts to come down during your ride and you're unprepared, you have a choice to make. Decide to keep on going as though it weren't raining at all. Or, realize that you had better make some compromises to your training plan for that day. The rain will affect you whether you choose to be reasonable or not.

The first thing that you may notice in the rain is that the street has taken on a wondrous wash of color. Beautiful pools and swirls of rainbow glistening from bright yellow past the happy greens through the moody shades of blue and into rich reddish hues. You haven't ridden through a looking glass or into Oz. Simply into a shimmering sheen of spilled gas, oil, and urban runoff. This pretty slick of petroleum products might cause you to lose traction, especially during the first hour of rain. The street will remain very slippery until the rain has fallen enough to wash all the hydrocarbons clean from the pavement and down into the storm drains where they will only be a problem for any living thing downstream. Any painted surface such as lane markings, crossing stripes, pedestrian crosswalks, or turn arrows will remain very slick once wetted by the rain. Same with anything metallic, like sewer caps. Puddles are fun to splash through as you ride, but not so much of a good time when the potholes that lurk under them reach out to take a bite out of your wheel. Avoid them when you can.

Rain causes other people to act strangely. So slow yourself down. Well-mannered pedestrians will scatter pell-mell into the streets once the first drop of rain pelts their paper shopping bags. Tourists will hit their brakes as though the rain were acidic. Trucks will blast their horns with disapproval. And most car drivers will just be looking to get to their destinations, so they won't be looking for cyclists. As a cyclist, you must remain calm in the storm while others around you lose their heads. The smartest thing would be to roll under the warm canopy of a coffee shop and enjoy a pleasant macchiato with extra whipped cream and caramel drizzled on top (have you noticed I kind of like coffee shops?). But I personally find riding in the rain exhilarating.

Because you're so dedicated to your plan, or you're in a really scary neighborhood where hubcaps on the cars are as scarce as a full set of teeth on the pedestrians, then I would move left as far as possible from the curb. Since most streets are paved with some idea of drainage in mind, the highest and driest part of the road will be toward the center. Streets are built so that rain and all the small fragments like cigarette butts, bottle caps, and bits of broken taillights will drain to the gutter. Riding close to the center not only will give you a drier and cleaner riding surface, you'll also have less of a chance of getting splashed from the deepening puddles that will be building from the gutters on out. There's also a good chance you'll be riding faster than traffic.

Keep in mind that if you have to use your brakes, unless you're on a mountain bike with discs, the brakes won't work as well until the pads wipe the rainwater from the rims. Once the brake pads do get a bite on the rim, they may sink in all of a sudden without warning. You don't want to endo in front of a soccer mom in an SUV. She may feel threat-ened and have to run over you in self-defense. Skidding through city or suburban intersections is not a good idea, either. So go easy on the braking. Traction is obviously not reliable on those skinny-ass tires.

Be grateful if you're wearing any kind of eyewear. Riding through pellets of falling rain can be painful without them. If you don't have eyewear, then you should consider riding your bike very defensively since your depth perception and field of vision have been severely compromised by extreme squinting.

Be mindful if you have been caught unprepared during a rain shower that if you continue to ride, your body temperature can quickly get chilled to the point where you may not be able to ride to-morrow. You'll start to get cold, and as you do, you'll begin to ride slower as your body works harder to keep itself warm than it does to ride fast. Try not to underestimate the distance to shelter. If you're out in the countryside where there is no place to pull over to stay warm, and you decide to ride on, watch out for signs of hypothermia.

- Uncontrollable shivering

- Exhaustion

- Grayish white skin color

- Loss of memory and mental confusion

- Loss of sensation of the extremities: fingers, toes, ears, and nose

- Drowsiness and the growing sense that the best thing you can do in this situation is curl up in the middle of the street and take a restful nap

If you can make your way to a—you guessed it—coffee shop, you should be able to treat yourself for mild signs of hypothermia if you have the presence of mind.

- Just breathing in warm, dry air will do much to elevate your core body temperature.

- Get dry and stay out of the wind and rain.

- Wrap yourself with whatever insulating material is on hand, e.g., dry newspapers, cardboard boxes, scraps of cloth.

- If you're riding with a buddy, huddling together increases the warming effect of body heat.

- If you're alert and able to swallow, drink warm fluids.

If you have any clue that there is a chance of rain before you set out, there are a couple of things that you can do to prepare. A waterproof shell jacket takes up almost no space when folded and can easily fit in your back pocket. Wear your gloves and booties as you go out the door. If the likelihood of rain is great, a pair of fenders will do a much better job of keeping you dry than you could ever imagine. But fenders don't look cool on a slick, whippy, expensive road machine. Some folks insist a red and drippy nose, thoroughly soaked chamois, and tire spray from the crack of your butt all the way up to the base of your helmet looks way cooler.

When I wake in the morning and I know that the whole day will be rainy or snowy, I just get on my mountain bike for my road ride. Sometimes I run slicks, but most times I keep the knobbies on. Even though it is a full-suspension bike, I am much happier pedaling it on a rainy road ride than I would be on a skinny-tire bike. Hidden potholes don't scare me. I can hop up on curbs if a car looks out of control. The disc brakes work better. The larger tire surface gets better traction even on wet pavement, especially if I let some of the air pressure out.

COLD

The best way to be prepared for cold weather riding is to practice exercising in the cold. Becoming accustomed to the extremes of weather is called acclimation. The body adapts to the extremes by either routing bloodflow to the internal organs to maintain body heat or by increasing bloodflow to the capillaries of the extremities and the skin's outer surface area in order to throw off excess heat.

When it's really cold, you can maintain your core body temperature by maintaining a high cadence. But make sure you don't bonk . . . or it will be a long, slow ride home. Although you might not feel the need, it's important to eat and drink while riding in the cold. You'll need this fuel for your muscles to burn so that you can keep warm. Be sure to wear underlayers of clothes that have the ability to wick away your body's sweat. The best insulation comes in layers. As a defense against hypothermia, a few thin shirts are more effective than a thick jacket at keeping you warm, especially if the clothing materials are made with polypropylene, not cotton blends. Damp clothing soon feels wet. Wet becomes cold even quicker. A ventilated outer layer is essential to vent the buildup of heat and perspiration. A windproof jacket front, with vents under the arms and at the back, is best. Use the jacket's zipper as a thermostat in order to control heat buildup.

Keep an eye on the time. Riding when the sun is high in the sky is the most opportune. Wait until it warms up the day, like during lunchtime, but time your ride so that before the sun begins to cast shadows, you're done for the day. Shadows easily distort vision and obscure road hazards. Cyclists often appear invisible to motorists in the darkness at only 4:30 on a winter afternoon.

The wind chill factor cannot be ignored when gauging the temperature that you'll be riding in. At, let's say, 40 degrees, factor in how cold you'll feel when riding at 15 mph . . . with a 10 mph crosswind! If possible, ride into the wind when you start out. That way as you come home, tired and cold, the wind and most of its effects are behind you.

Your hands, feet, and head will feel the cold the most. It may be hard to fit a wool cap under a helmet, but there are cycling-specific skull caps and balaclavas that work well. Mittens are better than gloves at keeping the fingers warm. Three-finger gloves are the best option for braking and shifting. Look for gloves with long cuffs or sleeves that can protect your wrists and forearms. Otherwise, use a jacket that's a size or two larger than you would normally wear so that you have good overlap at the wrist. Wool socks may require that you wear "winter" bike shoes that also are a size larger. The extra pair of winter shoes are really worth the expense, because once your toes begin to get cold, there isn't much you can do to warm them up again. When choosing these shoes, make sure they're compatible with a pair of waterproof booties.

HEAT

Acclimation works for hot weather, too. So the best way to learn how to deal with the heat is to ride in it often. This is a gradual process during which you should moderate your intensity a notch and reduce the duration of your rides.

Again, the time of day is an important factor. Noon is not a good time for hot-weather riding. It's cooler in the evening, but black pavement throws off a lot of residual heat, which you will feel on your bike hours after the sun sets. Much better to ride in the early morning when it's cool. In severe situations, like Las Vegas for instance, predawn rides may be necessary. As you get used to the heat, you can schedule your rides closer to the noon hour.

Drink before, during, and after your ride. In extreme conditions, in 1 hour of zone 3, you can lose up to 2 quarts of fluids. Dehydration is a great risk. To fight it, replenish every 15 minutes by drinking some sports drink containing the proper mixture of carbohydrates and electrolytes. Set your watch or bike computer to beep at intervals to remind you when it's time to drink. Sodium loss, which can lead to the inability to uptake fluids, can be mitigated by the intake of an electrolyte-rich sports drink and by foods that are sodium rich like pretzels and bagels.

You can freeze your sports drinks in their water bottles, leaving enough room for expansion, the night before you ride. Cool liquids not only are more refreshing, they help lower your core body temperature and are absorbed quicker.

Heat stroke or hyperthermia occurs when the body can no longer regulate its own temperature, and you in effect transform from a warm-blooded creature into a cold-blooded one with disastrous results. Do not allow yourself to exceed a body temperature of 102°F.

Without a thermometer, which every cool tool no matter how

cool still seems to lack, danger signs that you're overheating or approaching heat exhaustion are:

- Muscle cramping

- Fainting

- Exhaustion

Danger signs that you're hyperthermic are:

- Cessation of sweat

- Skin becomes hot to the touch and dries out

- Possibly feeling cold

Dave's Training Log— Week 12

Date	Sleep/Wt.	Workout	Notes
Mon	7 hrs/169		
Tue	8 hrs/167		(no time to ride)
Wed	8 hrs/168		
Thu	9 hrs/169		(nice 2 hr hike with Lorena and kids)
Fri	6 hrs/170		
Sat	8 hrs/169	1.5 hrs	Rode in Frederick with Marla; worked on climbing and descending stuff
Sun	8 hrs/168		

Total Riding Hours: **1.5**
Total Miles: **23**

• Vomiting

• Disorientation and headache

• Passing out

Emergency treatment is to seek shade or air-conditioning. Race Across AMerica (RAAM) riders famously seek the walk-in freezers of supermarkets or large restaurants when they find themselves in trouble. I've actually fallen asleep in one of these supermarket walk-ins. It was very comfortable.

Marla's Training Log— Week 12

Date	Sleep/HR/Wt.	Workout	Notes
Mon	9 hrs/47/140	2 hrs: zones 1–2	
Tue	9 hrs/ 43/140	1.5 hrs: zones 3–4 hill repeats— 5x5 min efforts	Felt great Stopped by Dave's
Wed	9 hrs/46/139	1 hr: zone 2	Easy, flat ride
		2 hrs: zone 3	Strenuous trail digging
Thu	6 hrs/46/140	1 hr: zone 2	Easy ride
Fri	8 hrs/45/140	3.5 hrs: zones 2–4	Big group ride; lots of energy, rode well
Sat	6 hrs/49/139	1.5 hrs: zones 2–3	Good road ride with Dave; worked on climbing, etc.
Sun	7 hrs/50/140	1.5 hrs: zones 3–4	Nice, hilly ride
Total Hours: **14**			

DAY 85 THROUGH 91 . . .
THE PRERIDE, NUTRITION,
AND THE TAPER

CHAPTER
13

"Your Century Ride starts at 10:00 A.M. on Saturday. That's June 12th, right?"

"Yup. The good old Southern Maryland Multiple Sclerosis Century Ride. Just rolls off the tongue, doesn't it?"

"Oh yeah, they all do. That's just 2 weeks, more or less. Perfect. You'll be tapered and ride ready."

"Yeah, I'm excited. Lorena and the kids are excited. I promised them that afterward we would all go "downy" ocean for a couple of days and search the beach for some shark teeth."

"That sounds like a plan."

We were riding side by side down Old Harford Road. Old Harford Road is the most direct route from the downtown of Baltimore where the Inner Harbor washes up against the new condos and the old row homes of Fells Point, to my mom and dad's house near the rock-strewn Gunpowder River. As we were pedaling past the tree-lined neighborhoods with slate-roofed houses, I thought it was strange how some things change and yet some other things stay the same. When I was a kid, I always thought the houses on this street must belong to "rich" people. The lawns were always so tidy and straight. The wood-sided station wagons and the black sedans were sitting proudly on their parking pads. The bright red brick and painted wooden trim of their vaguely Federal and Colonial mix all seemed so big back then. They were larger than my grandparents' home in the city where we had to park on the street when we visited. It didn't seem to make a difference to me then that these houses on Old Harford Road were smaller than the house that my dad had built for us out in Glen Arm. And our house was only wooden, no brick. And we had to shovel our long driveway in the winter. But now, spinning past these houses on Old Harford Road with Dave, I couldn't help but notice how small they are. They used to be huge! When I was a kid, my mom used to make it a great show when my dad brought home the thinly sliced corned beef and pastrami and braunschweiger from the Jewish deli on Lombard Street, which is not far from the Fells Point row home that Marc and I have just started to rehab. My mom put her hand over her heart when I told her how much we paid to buy that row home that needs much more than just the drop ceilings removed, the brick walls exposed, and the new stainless steel appliances squeezed inside.

That deli was the only place from which we bought our corned beef. It was a big deal because my dad had to go into the city to buy it. My parents didn't even like to drive through the city, instead preferring to drive around it on the 695 beltway. And just this afternoon, Dave and I had ridden right past that same deli on our way back out to our parents' house. What used to be an onerous and slightly dangerous car trip for my dad, Dave and I were enjoying as recreation on our bikes. These houses that I once thought opulent, which my parents were eager to leapfrog over, are soon going to be the next hot area to be reclaimed, revitalized, and rebuilt by a new generation who prefers walking and cycling over driving. I could easily recognize all this change. So how come it has taken me so long to realize that my brother, the guy who used to hold me down and send a long string of drool near my face and call me Rabbit because of my big front teeth, turned out to be such a good guy?

"Okay, Dave, just a couple things. I know you have always been pretty conscientious about your diet." And somehow he was. I don't know from where, because when we were kids at my mom's table, we learned that fish sticks, french fries, and buttered rolls covered all the food groups. He would have been even more lost if Lorena didn't come from a family where food was held in such iconic status. Lorena's house ate lots of organic fruits and vegetables, lots of olive oil, and real butter, but sparingly. Once or twice a week, they grilled or poached fresh fish caught in the ocean, not farmed in a tank. The kids snacked on carrots and thought plain white rice was a treat. But Dave, even if he had never met Lorena, would have somehow eaten healthfully anyway. Because eating healthfully makes sense. It's logical, and that's just the way Dave is.

"Tomorrow, while we're preriding something similar to your Century course, we'll talk about what you should be eating as you ride and how you taper off your training for a big day like that. Too bad we won't be preriding the exact same course because I don't have time to drive out there with you to do that. But I mapped out a 75-miler that begins and ends at Mount St. Mary's. The terrain is pretty similar. Sound okay?"

"Yeah, but if we aren't really riding the course, why don't we just ride 75 miles tomorrow starting from my house?" Dave really does depend on logic too much at times.

"Because we can't."

"You've said that, but why can't we? It would be a lot easier."

"There. That's why." It was fortunate for me, too, because I was just beginning to get frustrated and wasn't sure why. "Because that would be too easy for you. You know all the routes and roads and climbs and stuff near your house. This preride is supposed to prepare you for your big ride. You can't learn anything about how hard your Century

Ride will be if you preride a course where you already know all the surprises."

"Okay. I can see that." I knew where he was headed, so I cut him off—a little sister's prerogative.

"True, the best thing would be to drive out to the Blue Ridge Mountains. And with last year's course map, ride the exact course. Time sections of it. Note the difficult parts. Remember where the feed zones will be and stuff like that. But sometimes not even pros can preride an actual course. Tomorrow, Mount St. Mary's will be the next best thing. Besides, I know a really good brew pub there, for after we're done."

I went to college at Mount St. Mary's, so not only did I know from personal experience where there was indeed a very good brew pub, I knew where every dingy dive, every biker bar, and every local watering hole was, and even where the one gay bar was reputed to be within a hundred miles of the campus.

We were just reaching Putty Hill, where we would get off Old Harford Road. Soon after that, I'd take the quick right just after we crossed the bridge, to get to mom and dad's house for dinner. Mom had already told me that we were having crab cakes, one of dad's favorites. But I had in my messenger bag some salad fixings from Whole Foods, so there'd be more veggies. Dave would ride a few miles farther down Manor Road before he headed for his street, for his home, and for his healthy dinner.

The Preride

The first thing you can learn from preriding a similar course is an indication of your performance during your real Century Ride. With only a couple of weeks before your big day, you may not think that there is much you can do at this point training-wise to influence your performance during your Century Ride. Surprisingly, reliance on training sessions alone will never give you a good indication of how you'll perform on the big day. Up until now, your longest rides and most intense training sessions, even if they exceeded 100 miles, won't provide an accurate performance indication, because the conditions of these training sessions simply aren't similar enough to draw assumptions about how you'll do during your Century Ride. Will you bonk? And if so, where? Are the feed zones spaced too far apart? Can you easily carry and eat during your Century one dozen bananas as you hope to? How much water will you need to carry? Do you have all the right equipment?

The simplest way to find out those things and duplicate those conditions is to go ride the course. You don't have to ride the full 100 miles, but if you can without putting out too great an effort, that's great. If you think a full Century is too much, you should get a good idea from riding only 70 or 75 miles. Remember, you rode for 50 a few weeks back and that wasn't so bad (hopefully). Three-quarters of the way should provide a big-enough sample size for you to extrapolate your performance under actual conditions. As they are impossible to duplicate, the actual conditions can be approximated.

In order to prepare for the stages in the mountains of the 2004 Tour de France, where Lance Armstrong knew the race would be won or lost, Lance made a special trip to the base of those high peaks and he rode them. He did more than ride them. He tried to approximate the conditions that he would be under during the Tour. Just imagine: He would be days into the race already, tired, a little sore, under immense pressure. To prepare for that prior to preriding those mountain stages, he rode for days, hard and for comparable distances. And then he did climb mountains with some teammates, some of them playing the roles of his big competitors, Ullrich and Mayo. At which point during the climb should he expect the wind to blow cold? During those practice climbs he could fiddle with his gearing and with his bike setup. He would familiarize himself with how much he needed to hydrate and where during the climb he could wolf down an energy bar. Would the bar make him cramp? How many times would he have to urinate? He climbed for hours, and then because he knew that there was no way he could approximate the real race conditions of the Tour de

France when he got to the top, he went back down and climbed it once again. That's a pretty good approximation of the Tour's conditions, I imagine.

That's certainly one way to preride. You may not be able to do it quite like Lance did, but you should do it for the same reasons that he did: so you'll know what to expect on the big day, and so you'll know what you can expect from yourself as well. The greatest benefit of preriding the course, or trying as much as possible to duplicate the effort, is that the best training for riding 100 miles is simply riding 100 miles. All racers know that; that's why they say the best training is racing. Is there a reserve of strength there down deep after so many hours in the saddle that you know you can draw from? Has your butt ever been so sore in your life, and how will you deal with that?

Nutrition—On the Bike

It's difficult to anticipate what your nutritional needs will be during your Century Ride and even more difficult to find the best way to supply those needs.

Unless you have ridden for 5 or 6 hours at a stretch, one of the most difficult needs to imagine is nutrition. Start with your breakfast the day of the ride.

1. What should you eat?

2. How much should you eat?

3. When is the best time to eat it?

There are some general principles to guide you, such as a ratio between protein, carbs, and fats, but the best way to determine what's right for you is to go back over your training plan and look up what you ate before some of your big rides. If you see that the eggs Benedict and tomato juice caused some difficulty during the ride that followed, it's not a good idea to try that breakfast again on the morning of your preride. If you always have a bowl of oatmeal with an egg, then stick with that. Remember that the healthy diet that you have been enjoying lately got you to this point. So stick with it. If you know that you'll be riding for a long time and you have a tendency to bonk, I suggest eating a double-helping.

The timing of your meal is important. If my big event is scheduled for 9:00 a.m., then I do my preride at 9:00 a.m. I eat 3 hours prior to my preride just as I would prior to my big event. This allows for complete digestion. I adjust my sleep schedule so that by the day of my preride, I'll have enough of a window to eat my breakfast . . . and I try to stick to that schedule right up until the morning of my big event. I begin a little extra hydrating the day before my preride, as I would normally do the night before race day.

Try eating a hearty breakfast like a whole wheat bagel with cream cheese and a liquid meal like Endurox. Eggs are also great, but try to avoid greasy food. If you have been making your own smoothies with success up until now, stick with one of those. Just be sure to add a little protein and fat to all your carbs. Too many carbs alone before a big ride may cause a spike in your blood sugar levels, which could lead to a bonk just when you're calling out for more energy. You should have begun drinking lots of water the day before and continue to drink plenty right up until your event. If your urine is clear, that means that you're fully hydrated.

During the ride, drink and eat earlier than you think is necessary. Start drinking after you've been riding for about 30 minutes. Then take a gulp every 15 minutes or so. Usually the way it works for most people is that within 60 to 90 minutes of vigorous exercise, the body's quick and easy fuel source, glycogen, becomes depleted. After that time, your body starts to burn its fat stores. Sounds good, except that fat is hard to convert into energy that the muscles can use to power you through the rest of the ride. The conversion of fat comes at a high metabolic price, and your body is already being overtaxed. Look for energy bars that contain a little protein, too. A good ratio of protein to carb is 1 to 4. Eat around 75 grams of carbs—that's about one energy bar—every 30 minutes during your ride. However, if you haven't been eating, your glycogen is gone and since fat cannot be converted into energy, you'll slow down considerably and bonk. You should immediately refuel with carbs. Carbs are the easiest source of energy to be found in the back pocket of your jersey.

A more easily digested form of carbs can be found in the ketchup-style packets of Clif Shots. They are the best ones I've found and are easy to swallow during heavy breathing.

The easiest and quickest form of carbohydrates to digest is found in sports drinks (5 to 10 percent carbs net, 5 to 10 grams per milliliter). These carbs can be in any combination of simple or complex in form. Taken as a liquid, these carbs can be converted into fuel and used by the muscles within 15 to 20 minutes after drinking. Most of these sports drinks have a high sodium content as well, which helps prevent dehydration. They all contain various levels of other electrolytes, too. Sodium is the major one, but also important are potassium, chloride, and magnesium. These electrolytes ensure that the muscles contract, that the nerve impulses are transmitted, and that the most vital fluid level in the body, blood volume, is maintained. Because a little protein is also important to replenish, I prefer sports drinks like Endurox R4 and Accelerade. As long as you are good with a gram scale, you can add your own protein in the form of powdered whey, using a protein-to-carb ratio of 1 to 4, and mix up your own sports drink.

Some of these energy foods are more easily digested than others. Some taste better than others. Some are more expensive, and still others might not even be available to you in your area. For these reasons, during your training rides, it would have been a good idea to experiment to determine what works best for you. You may find that the old-fashioned energy bars, Bit-O-Honey or 3 Musketeers, suit you better. Some pro riders like nothing more than a warm, flat Pepsi as a sports drink. Some I know swipe the small packages of honey that you find in coffee shops, and they swear that they are the best sources of easy energy available.

Nutrition is as crucial to a successful Century performance as it is to basic training and health. When you ride, most of the fuel being

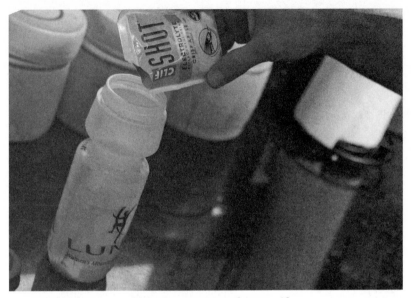

Be sure to add some sports drink mix to your water for every ride.

burned or oxidized is consumed by your active muscles. Just as a car needs gasoline to run, our bodies need fuel to run. The three fuel sources are carbohydrates, fats, and proteins. Proper fluid consumption during your ride is also essential.

CARBS

Carbohydrates are the primary and preferred fuel source for any activity. They are stored in the form of long chains of glucose molecules called glycogen in the muscles and liver. Carbohydrates must be replaced after about 60 to 90 minutes of riding, as muscle glycogen depletes quickly. To extend your energy reserves, you can do one of two things. One, don't exceed zone 2, or an aerobic pace. Or two, you can just keep taking in the carbs.

During a Century, you'll burn from 500 to 800 kcal (calories) per hour. Your body can store only 1,500 to 2,500 kcal, so 3 or 4 hours of riding will quickly deplete these stores (see "Bonking"). If there are lots of hills or you're putting out some good efforts, you may start to

BONKING

This term refers to the feeling that can occur when your body runs out of fuel or you become hypoglycemic. It feels just like someone bonked you over the head. Some people call it hitting the wall.

Here are some symptoms.

- Dizziness
- Confusion
- Nausea
- Slowed pace
- No power
- Irritability

This condition can occur easily when a rider is going anaerobic by riding intensely or climbing hard in the hills. The more intense the exertion, the more rapidly glycogen is depleted. Glycogen is the only fuel that can support efforts at above 70 percent of your max heart rate.

So when you bonk, your body will start to dip into your fat and protein stores, and you'll only be able to go at a slower, aerobic pace. Work must be reduced to about 50 percent of your max. Not only is this condition uncomfortable, it's detrimental to your muscles and central nervous system.

If this occurs too frequently, it will be difficult to finish your training sessions, and when it persists over several weeks, overtraining can develop.

To beat the bonk, you have to keep up with the carbs. Sip your energy drink every 15 minutes. Eat your gels or nibble some food every 30 minutes.

bonk after 1 or 2 hours. You burn much more glycogen going hard! As exertion increases linearly, muscle glycogen is depleted exponentially.

A 150-pound person burns about 500 kcal per hour while exercising, or 125 grams of carbs (each carb has 4 calories). So this person has to eat or drink at least 250 kcal per hour to keep riding efficiently.

Energy drinks (with 5 to 8 percent carbs in water) like Accelerade or Cytomax turn carbohydrates into energy quicker than food, because they're absorbed from the stomach faster. So it's a good idea to drink a few gulps every 10 to 15 minutes, or a bottle an hour. Gels like Clif Shots are also extremely effective when taken with water. A shot every 30 minutes is recommended.

After about 30 minutes of riding, try to eat frequently as well. Food carbohydrates are more complex and burn longer. I find organic energy bars like Clif Bars or Luna Bars are the best choice because of their great taste, extensive nutrient profile, and convenient packaging for your jersey pocket. Energy bars pack a big carbohydrate punch and usually provide extra vitamins and minerals. Other good options are bagels, fig bars, bananas, and raisins.

FATS

In general, the longer the ride, the greater the role fat plays as a fuel. Although there are relatively large fat stores in the body, fat is still oxidized slowly during exercise. Theoretically, fat in the adipose tissue of the average person could provide energy for days. So if you're thinking about losing a few pounds of body weight, consider getting rid of that extra fat.

Your strength-to-weight ratio influences cycling performance, especially in the hills. If weight reduction is one of your goals, it's important to maintain a negative energy balance by eating less fat in your diet and exercising longer and harder. Fat oxidation must exceed fat intake. What a surprise!

To lose that extra fat:

• Record your body weight daily and set realistic goals.

• Ride longer at 60 to 70 percent max HR to burn more fat.

• Be careful with your on-the-bike drinking strategy—each liter of sports drink adds about 300 calories. Alternate these with water.

• Go for gradual weight reductions—about a pound a week. Too much too fast is unhealthy and won't last long.

- Eat more whole grains, vegetables, fruits, and balanced meals.

- Don't eat after 8:00 P.M.

- Avoid fried or overprocessed foods with trans fats.

- Make sure 15 to 20 percent of your daily calories come from healthy fats, found in foods like olive oil, avocados, and fish.

- Always eat high-carb foods right after hard training.

- Keep healthy snacks around the house to avoid fatty temptations.

In order for weight loss to be maintained, these changes in your exercise and diet habits need to become a part of your lifestyle. The most successful athletes are those who reasonably modify their diet and reduce excess fat intake, record their body weight regularly, exercise regularly and often, and receive a lot of support from their friends and family.

If your weight seems to stay the same even during increased training, changes in your body composition may be occurring, where you have a higher muscle-to-fat ratio. The resulting elevated metabolic rate will also help you maintain your weight.

PROTEIN

The amino acids that make up protein are essential for muscle synthesis, hormones, connective tissue, and enzymes. Protein can also serve as an energy source when available glycogen and fat stores are low. A 165-pound person requires about 60 grams of protein a day. Most Americans get this in their diets easily without thinking about it.

Cyclists may require more protein during periods of increased riding or time in the gym, so that 165-pound guy may need to consume an extra 75 to 100 grams of protein a day. The best way to do this is with natural food products like fish, meat, dairy, or legumes. For convenience, there are also some great high-protein bars out there like Clif Builder's bars. Protein supplementation in the form of high-tech powders and various forms of amino acid supplements can be effective, albeit expensive.

The time to supplement is when you're off the bike. When riding, avoid eating foods with more than 15 percent protein. They're tougher to digest; your urine output will increase; and you'll run the risk of becoming dehydrated.

Hydration

Water is the single largest component of a cyclist's body, so it makes sense that proper fluid consumption before, during, and after training is a necessity. One of the most common mistakes is for riders to become dehydrated, resulting in an obscene reduction of performance and potential heat injury. It's important to drink extra water 2 days leading up to a Century. Learn to monitor your fluid status by checking your urine. The more clear and frequent, the better.

On hot days, riders can lose up to a quart, or 2 pounds, of fluid an hour through sweating and breathing. This leads to a progressive rise in temperature and sets you up for premature fatigue and risk of heatstroke. Whether you're drinking water or a sports drink, you should take a gulp every 10 to 15 minutes, or a bottle an hour. A hydration system worn on your back is very effective to help you replenish fluid lost. Most of these systems hold between 70 and 100 ounces.

Sweat loss also results in a loss of electrolytes (minerals), the principle one being sodium. The need for replacing electrolytes during and after exercise has been well documented, thus the invention of the slightly salty Gatorade.

Nutrition—Off the Bike

Setting up your preride so that it's as close as possible to the real thing will confirm the best breakfast to have before your Century. It will also give you some idea of what on-the-bike nutrition works best for you during your 100 miles.

But a healthy diet and proper nutrition *off* the bike is the foundation on which any goal in cycling rests, not just riding 100 miles. That's why it may seem out of place to talk about nutrition "off the bike" so late in this book. Wouldn't it have been better to discuss the role nutrition plays in planning for a Century ride earlier in the process? If it is the foundation on which the rest of the training is built, shouldn't nutrition then be the first chapter?

I knew back when I was in my late twenties, when all I wanted to do was be a pro cyclist, that diet was important. What girl didn't already know that? Guys are oblivious to some things, but from an early age all girls know a lot about diet. Boys, if they're above average, think that The Diet is the name for the legislative body in some other countries. If they aren't above average, all they know about The Diet is that their sister worries about it all the time, which is a mystery to them because otherwise their sister evidences no interest at all in foreign political affairs.

It took a while, but after I was a pro for a few years, I realized that I had been overemphasizing the importance of diet at the expense of my training. My diet had become my primary concern. Rather than eating so that I could ride stronger or faster or longer, I began to ride so that I could stick to my diet. It got all mixed up. Sometimes I would find myself altering the length or intensity of a training ride because I knew that I didn't have the strength or energy to finish it. Breakfast after all had been a dry bagel, and some coffee, no cream or sugar. There were plenty of rides that I cut short because I hadn't eaten enough. I thought the key to being a top climber was to be as skinny as a rail. I learned the hard way that being skinny can hurt your power-to-weight ratio more than it helps.

Needless to say, as my riding suffered, I became more vigilant about sticking to my diet. That salad dressing should have been on the side, not tossed all over the lettuce! This downward spiral may sound familiar to women, but completely alien to men. The reasoning, although fractured, is easy to appreciate. Diet is one of the few things over which one has absolute control.

You can't control the cost of a college education for the kids. You have no control over the cost of insurance, housing, or gasoline. You might not even feel like you have any say in who becomes president. But you can control what you eat. So you do that.

It's tempting to control what you eat rather than wrestle with trying to squeeze in the time to ride your bike. You can select exactly what kind of food you eat, whereas you are powerless to stop the rain from cutting short your ride. You can determine how many calories you'll consume, but you can do nothing about the shrinking daylight of winter that cuts into your afternoon mileage.

It took me a few years to straighten out all this topsy-turvy diet stuff. That's why now I eat to ride, not ride to eat. I am not haphazardly just winging my workouts, but instead I'm implementing a well-thought-out training program. I'm charting out a periodization plan for my training that is comprised of establishing a baseline, and from there setting a realistic goal, then building up my fitness through progressive training loads, tapering to a peak performance, and then enjoying a recovery period. I'm following that periodized method of training both on a micro and a macro scale. I am not overtraining, and I remain injury-free through diligence and self-control. Well, I try anyway. I am listening to my body, asking it to do only what it's capable of and allowing it to recover as necessary. I am getting the proper sleep and maintaining a positive mental attitude. If I'm doing all these things, then naturally, without much effort and without ever realizing it, I also would have been likely following a healthy diet.

So now if I have planned to go for a long ride during the afternoon, I eat a hearty breakfast and a light lunch that will provide me energy so that I can withstand the stresses on my body during that ride. During that ride if there is a need for a Clif Bar or a powdered sports drink, I satisfy that need. After that ride, I eat what my body needs to recover from my exertions. Dinner that night is not fried. The portions aren't huge. The sauce's main ingredient likely won't be heavy cream or a stick of butter, but if the rare occasion arises that it is, I skip dessert. Alcohol in moderation, and not too much coffee.

You'll find after a couple of weeks of regularly riding your bike, regardless of the eating habits you might have had, you'll want to eat a more healthful diet. Before an afternoon ride, you won't feel the urge to eat $10 worth of fast food. Okay, you might do that just out of old habit, but the result will be so unpleasant that you'll be unlikely to eat that way again.

Just listen to what your body is telling you.

After that long ride, you may certainly feel a need for quick calories, something salty and starchy. It's not just coincidence that even the best riders in the world after a summer afternoon in the hills crave a big, doughy salted pretzel and a cold amber ale. But they have only one, maybe two, because they know their bodies want to be ready for tomorrow's ride.

That's the only diet you really need to follow. Just eat to recover from today's ride and to prepare for tomorrow's ride. Eating is even easier than riding a bicycle. Or so it seems.

The Taper

The taper is the part of your periodized training where you cease the progressive loading of your rides.

You don't change your hours of sleep. You keep constant the kinds and number of meals that you have been eating. You just don't train as much, so your appetite might also decrease. The taper is a marked decrease in intensity and duration from your training levels in order to prepare you for the big effort of your Century Ride. By doing so, the taper ensures that you have an adequate recovery from all that heavy training. And that you're fresh as a daisy and champing at the bit.

That's right—a recovery even before you ride your hundred miles. You need to recover at this point, because all the hard work is behind you. You should recover from all those miles, and you should know that simply riding 100 miles will be easy.

A taper is not a free pass to just stop riding. You still ride on the days that you normally would. You still start your rides at the time you have customarily done so; you just reduce the mileage or the time in the saddle anywhere from 25 to 50 percent. If you just want to finish your first Century, then you should make a reduction of around 25 percent. If you want to bury the rest of the field, if you really think you want to win and you want to go all out, then reduce your training load by up to 50 percent. Introduce your reductions gradually, not all at once. Remember, you progressively loaded your training, so you should successively reduce it so that by the morning of your Century Ride, you're in peak physical and mental condition.

A good time to start your taper for a one-time event like a Century Ride is right after finishing your preride. If you have been sticking close to your original 100-Day Training Plan, you have about a week or two until you need to peak for your Century. Perfect timing.

On the day following your preride, you may be a little stiff. That's normal. Walk off any little aches, stretch out any creaky joints. Swim. Go for a quick, easy spin. Do whatever you normally do on your easy day. You can look forward to your next training day, because you won't be riding as long as you have been. This is the start of your taper. Enjoy it.

Although there will be a reduction in training load, you'll be trying to ride faster on your hard days. For instance, if you have been riding 3-minute intervals for 8 reps as part of your intensity workout, you should now reduce your intervals to 2 minutes and do only 6 reps. But try to go faster. During your next interval day, again reduce the duration of your intervals, this time to 1 minute, and again reduce the number of intervals to 4 reps. But again try to ride harder or faster. Keep this routine of reductions up until the day before your Century. The day before, go for a quick spin—45 minutes or so—and you should feel like a superhero ready to burst through your chamois.

If you have been training for this particular Century Ride as a way to supplement or jump-start your normal cycling training, enjoy your taper as well. You might shorten the depth or decrease the strength of the taper, because afterward you'll presumably continue a season of racing toward your goals.

Dave's Training Log— Week 13

Date	Sleep/Wt.	Workout	Notes
Mon	8 hrs/168		
Tue	8 hrs/168		
Wed	8 hrs/168	1 hr: Easy spin	Felt fine
Thu	7 hrs/168		
Fri	7 hrs/169		
Sat	9 hrs/168	5 hrs: Big preride near Mount St. Mary's	Pretty long day; went easy to moderate; tried to eat and drink a lot
Sun	10 hrs/168		

Total Riding Hours: **6**
Total Miles: **106**

Marla's Training Log— Week 13

Date	Sleep/HR/Wt.	Workout	Notes
Mon	8 hrs/47/140	2 hrs: zones 1–2	
Tue	9 hrs/43/140	1.5 hrs: zones 3–4 Hill repeats— 5x5 min efforts	Felt great
Wed	9 hrs/49/139	1 hr: zone 2 2 hrs: zone 3 upper body in gym	Easy, flat ride
Thu	6 hrs/46/140	1 hr: zone 2	Easy ride
Fri	9 hrs/45/140	3.5 hrs: zones 2–4	Big group ride; lots of energy; rode well
Sat	6 hrs/49/139	1.5 hrs: zones 2–3	Good road ride
Sun	7 hrs/50/140	1.5 hrs: zones 3–4	Nice group ride
Total Hours: **14**			

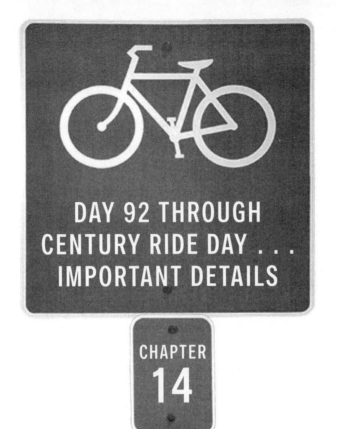

DAY 92 THROUGH CENTURY RIDE DAY . . . IMPORTANT DETAILS

CHAPTER 14

"You were pretty strong last week on that long ride. I bet now after a good taper, I'd have to practically hold you back, huh?"

"I wouldn't go as far as saying that. Modesty precludes me. But the way I feel now is great! I wish now that Chris wasn't just talking smack about jumping in and riding this thing, too. I'd love to look back at him and smile as I dropped him right on the first climb. You're so right, I'm ready to rip. I just hope I'll feel this way on Saturday morning."

"Don't worry, you will."

"Lorena is pretty psyched, too. I suspect she thought at first that I wasn't up for it. But she's turned out to be a really great partner in all this. She said the other day that it's been inspiring for her to watch me put this whole training plan into action. She said it's even made her think about setting up an office in downtown Baltimore, you know, something she always thought she'd never be able to pull off."

"That's great, Dave! You see? Told ya. You do one impossible thing and then all the other impossible things don't seem so hard."

Lorena is right. I'm proud of her, too. But I felt some sadness about not being there with Dave at the end for his big ride. It was midweek. I was already on the road racing mountain bikes weekend after weekend. Dave had told me that ultimately he was going to have to do all the pedaling himself. That there was only so much I could do for him, and I had done a lot, he'd told me. Still, I really felt like I was missing out on something.

Those rides with Dave had really changed things for me. They made me realize how lucky I've been to have bike riding as a big part of my life. I don't know how he had been living without a bike ride every now and then. He must have been going crazy and not even knowing it. I know I would have. Helping him get on his bike clued me in to how much getting on a bike had been helping me. And that was important to me now. Especially now as I was just starting out on my last season as a downhill specialist. Maybe.

You never know what's down the road. That's one of the best things about riding a bike.

Living in Baltimore once again after so many years away was a big change. I loved the time spent doing things with my family, like picking out and setting up a Christmas tree. And then debating over which of us was going to break it down and drag it to the recycling center. Seeing the old places like the Charles Theatre, and late night coffee at the Café Hon. Sneaking back into Mount St. Mary's to swipe a quick shower after poaching some trails near the campus. It was better than old times. Maybe it's just my biological clock ticking, but living here where I grew up has been making me think about settling down. It's brought out some nurturing qualities. Small ones, I admit, that I never knew I had.

"Dave, have you gone on the Web to that weather site? It always rains on me when I go on these kinds of rides. You can get pretty cold out there."

"Yeah. Got that site up on the corner of my desktop. Do you want to know how many millibars the air pressure has dropped over the last 24 hours? Within a 5-mile radius of feed station #2?"

"Okaaay. Sounds like you've got a handle on it. You've got some waterproof stuff, right?"

"I do. I'm all set. And I'm excited. The boys are excited, too. They see me at all their basketball games and soccer matches. They know I'm a wallflower during their dancing lessons and that I'm biting my nails during their chess club meetings. And they've told me that they finally get to cheer me on. Evan said he's actually nervous. He told Lorena that he's afraid that I may be putting too much pressure on myself. Can you believe that?"

I could. Evan is mature beyond his years in many ways. That's a pretty serious insight to have concerning your dad at any age. He's only 10. "When you ride past him, show him you're having a blast. Moon him or something."

"Is that pro advice?"

"You know what I mean."

"I'll give them a big smile. How's that?"

"Sounds better."

Dave let me go after a few more minutes of chitchat. He knew I wanted to hike up to inspect the downhill course. Before we said good-bye, though, I made him promise me that he'd call on Friday night, so I could give him a last-minute pep talk.

I had to bite my tongue. The desire was so strong to tell him how proud I was of him for working so hard all spring. And how happy I was for him that he was really going to do this, ride a Century. But we Strebs are reserved. A little more quiet when it comes to talk like that. So, as I laced up my hiking shoes and slipped on my Team Luna cap to keep the sun out of my eyes as I hiked up the hill, I only allowed myself a smile. Dave was going to have a ball and maybe a sore butt, sure. In the fall when my mountain biking season was over, Dave would be there all primed and ready to ride. Maybe then we could do a Century Ride together? One of those colored-leaves classics in New England?

We definitely gotta get Chris on the program next year.

The week before your Century Ride, you still have some details to attend to. You have done all the hard work. The big rides are behind you; only the fun ride ahead of you. But to make sure everything goes smoothly, you should go through a checklist.

1. Get a tune-up for the bike.

2. Double-check any travel arrangements.

3. Make sure your registration for the ride is in.

4. Check and pack your equipment.

Sometimes you're so focused on your ride that you forget some of the small things that you need in order to pull it off. Giving your bike a tune-up is one of those things. You're tapering right now. That means that your bike isn't being ridden as much this week as last. Your bike needs to be just as ready as you for your Century. But it's only a jumble of tubes, shiny parts, and greasy bits. It can't derive any beneficial rest from just leaning up against the garage wall.

Set aside some of the free time you now have because you're in your taper. On one of those days during this last week, use that second hour that you normally spend riding to tune up your bike. Choose a time earlier in the week as opposed to later in the week. Friday afternoon is not a great time to drop your bike off at the shop expecting to pick it up early in the morning all tuned, lubed, and ready to ride. Even if your bike shop has never let you down before, why risk months of training because the shop's head mechanic never made it back to the wrench room that day from his lunchtime ride? First time ever.

If you work on your bike yourself, Friday afternoon is also not a good time to clamp it in the stand and strip it down. You'll be astounded at how far across the floor a single BB from your headset will roll if you open it up to repack it with grease. Even if you've never done anything like that before, you'll snip a new length of shifter cable just a teensy bit too much so that your chain won't move up to your big ring. Just don't do it. That you find working on your bike meditative or relaxing is not a valid argument. Do that work earlier in the week. If you need a relaxing outlet the night before your Century, work on your partner's bike. Take apart the lawn mower. Find out once and for all why there's a whiny noise from your entertainment system's wireless speakers when the compressor in the refrigerator kicks in.

Just see to it that your bike's chain is cleaned and lubed. That the springs in your clipless pedals move freely. That there is no play in your headset. No nasty noises from your bottom bracket. Spin your wheels slowly, and make sure they're true. Spokes all tight? Check out your tires. Do the sidewalls look okay? How about the rolling surfaces—any nicks, slits, or shiny bits of glass? Zip it around the block and shift through all the gears. Just don't assume that it shifts well because the last time you rode it everything was fine, especially if you listen to music when you ride. The earphones can hide all sorts of stuff that you might not notice, like your chain rubbing against your front derailleur. After you're sure that it shifts smoothly and quietly, test the brakes. Good stopping power? No scary squealing? Plenty of pad left? Even if you normally have your favorite shop do all your work, go through your bike yourself, and write up a punch list of items that you think they should look at. If your shop is really managed well, your bike will be running fine when you get it back, and the shop will not have felt slighted about the paper dangling from the handlebar listing your items of concern.

Double-check your travel arrangements a few days ahead of your event. Are you flying? Will the airline accept your bike as a "roll-on" piece of luggage? In Europe most carriers allow you to simply roll your bike up to the ticket desk and then hang a luggage tag from the handlebar. It's easier for everybody if you remove the pedals from the cranks, drop your saddle as low as possible, and loosen your headset so you can spin your bar so that it's no longer perpendicular to the frame. That's not a big deal compared to what the domestic carriers ask of you.

Most domestic airlines will not allow you to roll your bike on. They will ask that your bike be boxed. In the past, I have used special bike boxes, both hard and soft. The boxes do a great job of protecting your bike during travel. The boxes have room for extra gear like spare tubes and tires, your helmet and shoes, floor pump, and miscellaneous tools. The bags do such a good job of neatly storing and protecting all this gear that you run into trouble when you try to check it. Most airlines classify bicycles as oversize luggage. That designation carries a surcharge. In addition to the surcharge is a weight limit of 50 pounds. If you exceed that weight limit, you will have to pay a penalty based on the excess poundage. Since 9/11, I have found it easier to pack my bike in one of the cardboard bike boxes that bike shops ship and receive their bikes in. The cardboard is not as durable, and it doesn't offer as much protection as the hard plastic or soft canvas bike bags do. But they do weigh significantly less, and they're a lot smaller, too, which means that you can't jam a lot of extra heavy equipment into them. With reinforcing duct tape, the cardboard bike boxes hold up well for a round-trip flight. But don't be surprised, when you pick up your bike from the oversize luggage bin at the airport, that the cardboard has been neatly slit with a knife. For security reasons, the bike boxes are often inspected. In addition to saving weight, don't put extra equipment like your bike shoes or helmet in the box, because after the box is opened by security, those items may tumble out and be lost during the rest of the flight. Don't bother trying to fly with CO_2 quick fill–type cartridges. They will be confiscated. Airlines aren't as interested in double-shot minipumps.

The airline check-in and baggage pickup process takes at least an hour each. There is always the risk of not arriving with your bike if you must take a connecting flight. Some of the smaller regional airports like Santa Barbara and San Luis Obispo that are near the very popular Solvang Century use only small turboprop planes. Those planes can squeeze in only a limited number of bike boxes. If, however, you are a member of USA Cycling, bike vouchers are available, which will save you the $50 surcharge that the airline normally assesses bikes. Even with that little bonus, I often find it easier to drive to an event if the driving will be under 8 hours. You often find a need to rent a car upon arrival anyway, because rarely are Century Rides staged within a short cab or bus ride of an airport.

Staying at a motel near the event? Why don't you call and ask on what floor your room is? Request a room close to the ground floor, or one in front of which you can park. Carrying a bike up a flight of stairs or in and out of an elevator is no fun. You should bring it inside your room, though. Leaving it inside your car or locked to a bike rack on the roof overnight may tempt local ne'er-do-wells. Good idea to double-check with the motel that your room is a nonsmoking one. You'll sleep much better the night before your ride.

Friday is also not the smartest time to check on your registration, especially from the Internet after business hours. Use another hour of free time courtesy of your taper on Monday or Tuesday to call the event organizer to make sure your registration was received in time. If the organizer has a problem because your payment check is out of state or your credit card number's digits have been transposed, you'll have a couple of business days to straighten out things.

If your organizer has sent you an information package on the event, have you read it? Now would be a better time than Friday night. Sometimes buried in those packets are critical pieces of information about where to pin your event number: on your back or chest, or zip tie it from the saddle or handlebar. The info packet may contain changes to the route or provide a great map of the route. The most critical piece of information to confirm from the packet is the starting time. As elemental as that sounds, I have driven hours, set up a tent in the dark, camped out the whole rainy night, warmed up the next morning and pedaled down the street arriving at the starting line on Sunday only to learn that the event was held on Saturday.

You should realize that many of these Century Rides are organized by volunteers as fundraisers for worthy causes. You really can't yell into the phone at the blue-haired lady on the receiving end because your info packet didn't contain complimentary zip ties that you expected to hang your number plate with. This is a Century Ride; the stakes aren't as great as the Tour de France. Relax. Similarly, because many of these Century Rides are organized by well-meaning volunteers, you shouldn't rely too heavily on their resources. If the info packet or Web site for the event says that the ride is fully supported with course marshals, feed stations every 25 miles, police escorts, sweeping sag wagons, and precision timing systems, don't be too upset when you discover all those things are in the eyes of the volunteer organizers.

A lot of these events are preceded by a traditional carbo-loading spaghetti dinner the night before. Depending on the event, the spaghetti dinner is held in the dining room of a host hotel, the cafeteria of the local hotel, or the backyard of the event promoter. The spaghetti eats are not only fun and a nice way to meet some of the people you'll be riding with, but they are a great way to get some indication about what you will be in for during your ride the next day. No forks with your pasta is an obvious clue.

There is some validity to carbo-loading as a way to prepare for a single long-distance event like a Century Ride. The normal percentage of carbs in the typical healthy diet is around 60 percent. But you are preparing for a Century Ride, so you may need some more complex carbs that you can draw from as fuel. A few days prior to your event, think about increasing your daily intake of carbs to 70 percent of your total daily calories (1 gram of carbohydrate equals 4 calories). If you increase your carbs to 70 percent during your taper, your reserves of glycogen will be topped off. Don't mind too much if after a few days of eating an extra helping of pasta, you begin to feel "heavy." This is just extra water weight, a small side effect of carbo-loading. The extra water will be sweated away soon enough during your Century. It's unlikely that you'll be negatively affected by it. The benefit of the extra energy from the carbs far outweighs any heaviness or bloating you may temporarily have to deal with.

The night before the event, don't get carried away. It's not a good idea to try to load all your carbs at one sitting.

Before you leave for the event, make sure you check that you have packed all your equipment. Write up a list of what you need. Keep that list handy. As you pack these items, check to make sure you haven't forgotten any.

- Helmet/eyewear

- Shoes/socks/gloves

- Chamois/jersey; jacket, if necessary

- Computer/heart rate monitor

- Sports drink/energy bars

- Hydration system/water bottles

- Patches/tube and pump/cool tool

- Bike

If you're staying at a motel or a friend's house the night before the event, unpack your gear. If anything is missing, you still have an opportunity to make some panicked phone calls. Before you crawl into bed for the night, lay all this stuff out in some orderly fashion. Some of these Century Rides start really early in the morning, and fumbling around in a strange motel room before dawn is an invitation to lose something. If you're driving from home the morning of the event, have your gear all packed neatly in a bag by the door the night before. That way, in the morning you can pick it up as you stroll out to the car with your coffee in the other hand.

On the Day of Your Century

Your preride should have clued you in to much of what you need today. If things went pretty well during your three-quarter distance ride, don't make any drastic changes today. If anything feels strange or out of place, it's probably just butterflies. If you had to wake up at the crack of dawn in order to get to the start on time, your body should have been gradually adjusting its sleep clock since your pre-ride so there will be no shock to your system.

Enjoy your breakfast. At least 3 hours before the event, if possible. Hydrate. Don't eat too much. Eat a large meal, but don't stuff yourself.

If you went to the spaghetti dinner the night before, you might have found out from other riders who have done this event in the past if it's well-organized or not. If it turns out that the organizer leaves some of the details up to you the rider, do something about that right now. Make sure you have a course map with you.

I prefer to keep a course map or directions stuck to the sleeve of my jersey like the enduro motorcycle riders do. You don't need a *National Geographic* topo map, but something better than a pencil drawing is nice. You can often download something from the Web site or tear off a half page from your info packet. Add to it anything special that you want to keep in mind that the map may lack—elevation, a bridge crossing, historical sites, important place names, a particular spot where you think it's a good idea for your partner to be cheering you on. You can just fold up the map and stick it in the back of your jersey, but I find that my maps often get ruined back there, gooey from energy bars and soft from sweating. Some riders stick their maps in a clear pocket on a bag mounted to the top of their handlebar. That's convenient, easy to see, safe from the elements, and probably a better idea than jamming your map into a small pocket somewhere on your hydration pack.

The best advice I could give Dave was that a Century Ride begins at the 50-mile mark. Up to that point, you're just rolling down the road with friends and meeting new people. Checking out the sights. You're barely even hungry by that point, only 2 or 3 hours into your ride. Your riding high kicked in a few miles back. Enjoy how strong you feel. Your legs can pedal forever it may seem; the taper, the carbo-loading, and all those miles earlier in the year are really paying off at this point. Just don't get too excited. Remember when you went on your first training ride? About the only thing you could do wrong then was to ride too hard. Same thing now for the same reason. Keep your speed reasonable. Don't exceed zone 2 or 3, unless you're racing. If you're using a heart rate monitor, don't exceed your anaerobic threshold for any length of time. I know it sounds crazy, but if you have followed your training plan, the hardest thing to do now during your ride is rein yourself in.

Take it easy and enjoy it.

If, however, you are motivated by the spirit of competition, if you feel like you want to put the hurt on some of your buddies that you have been training with, the 50-mile point is where you make your move. And it shouldn't be a big move. Nothing like putting the hammer down. You still have a long way to go. But with half the ride behind you now, you should have a pretty good feeling of what you're capable of for the rest of the day.

A good strategy at this point is to increase your intensity by 5 percent—your intensity, not your speed. If you have a heart rate monitor, increasing your intensity by 5 percent should be easy to accomplish. Without a heart monitor, you can come pretty close. Be careful not to make the mistake of confusing an increase in intensity with an increase in speed. They don't always correlate.

If you can maintain that increased intensity for the next 25 miles, and you think you have more in your tank, go for it. Increase your intensity another 5 percent for the next 15 miles, and then assess how you're doing. If you still feel strong at the 90-mile mark, by all means increase your intensity 5 percent more.

If, however, by the time you arrived at the 75-mile marker, you felt a little ragged, you can either decide to ride on as you have been at the same pace, or you can drop it down a notch. At this point, you are already three-quarters of the way through. You should have ridden this distance only a week or so ago. Another 25 miles should comfortably be within your reach. But sometimes, it turns out just not to be your day. Breakfast may not have settled well. The climbs were bigger than you anticipated. You may have been frustrated all morning with ghost shifting. Don't worry about it. That's all behind you, now. Just revel in the moment, enjoying the thought that a few hours from now, you will have ridden your bike 100 miles!

Dave's Training Log—
Week 14

Date	Sleep/Wt.	Workout	Notes
Mon	9 hrs/165	1 hr: easy spin	Good recovery
Tue	8 hrs/167		
Wed	8 hrs/168		(worked on bike)
Thu	8 hrs/168	1.5 hrs: moderate pace	Felt great
Fri	7 hrs/167		
Sat	9 hrs/168		
Sun	6 hrs/167	1.5 hrs	Went pretty hard, had lots of energy; ready for next week!!

Total Riding Hours: **4**
Total Miles: **73**

Marla's Training Log— Week 14

Date	Sleep/HR/Wt.	Workout	Notes
Mon	8 hrs/47/140		Travel day
Tue	9 hrs/43/140	1.5 hrs: zones 3–4 Hill repeats— 5x5 min efforts	Felt okay
Wed	9 hrs/49/139	1 hr: zone 2 2 hrs: zone 3 upper body in gym	Easy, flat ride
Thu	6 hrs/46/140	1 hr: zone 2	Easy spinnage
Fri	9 hrs/45/140	3.5 hrs: zones 2–4	Big group ride; tired, but rode well
Sat	6 hrs/49/139	1.5 hrs: zones 2–3	Good road ride
Sun	7 hrs/50/140	3.0 hrs total	Big race; got 3rd in finals

Total Hours: **13.5**

AFTER YOUR CENTURY RIDE

CHAPTER 15

Try not to grab a beer right after rolling across the line. It may sound good, but there are better sources of calories you should think of first. A smart way to think is that your Century isn't over until you're recovered from the day's efforts. The beer only replenishes two of the three items your body needs. You do need to top off your fluid stores. The beer does do that, but keep in mind that the alcohol in it acts as a diuretic, which means beer will make you even more dehydrated. You need to replace all the fluids that you lost during your ride and then add half as much again. That's a lot. Water works well, but you can facilitate the process by drinking some of the sports recovery drinks. After riding a Century, you need to retain fluids, plus electrolytes and glycogen.

There is only a brief opportunity to replace the depleted glycogen stores following such a long ride. You have about 30 minutes to consume healthy carbs, simple sugars, or glucose, which will rapidly replace the lost glycogen. Beyond 30 minutes consuming carbs helps, but the conversion to glycogen takes place less efficiently. Two hours after your ride, the ability of your body to refuel itself has greatly diminished.

Your carb source should be glucose or other simple sugars, because these carbs produce glycogen quickly. These simple sugars stimulate the production of insulin in the pancreas. The insulin makes it easier for the uptake of glycogen in the muscles. Insulin also stimulates the production of an enzyme called glycogen/synthetase, which speeds up the catalysis of glycogen from the simple sugars of the carbs. So after a big ride, more insulin means a faster rate of turning glucose into glycogen, which the muscles are starving for. But again, after 2 hours, this process nearly shuts down.

A small amount of protein helps, too. Again, go for the 4:1 ratio of carbs to protein.

This recovery ratio should not be overdone, though. You're still consuming calories. Beyond a certain point, too many carbs—more than 5 grams per pound of body weight—means that you no longer improve the production of glycogen, and you're just putting on weight. A pound or two isn't so bad after a long day of riding, but try to refrain from adding more.

So, wait at least 2 hours before having a beer. At that point, it can't hurt.

If you're hurting, that is if your muscles are sore or you experience swelling, a postride massage can be a good way to flush the edema through your system. Many times after events, massage therapists are on hand either volunteering their time or offering their services for a nominal fee. Massage therapists can only aid the process of flushing the soreness and swelling from your muscles. You, yourself, can do a large part of the job if you're able to walk around or ride easily to cool down before hopping onto the table. A cold shower, followed by warm water and then another cold rinse, works well too. If you can shower before climbing on the table, the massage therapist greatly appreciates that as well.

Very rarely there may be a need for RICE treatment. Rest, Ice, Compression, and Elevation is typically only called for after a rider has suffered an injury of some sort. Sometimes, a fall will cause bruising to an arm or leg and such treatment may be required. Severe blistering of the toes and feet, and less often the hands and fingers, may also benefit from this treatment.

A mild anti-inflammatory like Advil or Motrin can take some of the sting out of your soreness.

Take the time to thank the volunteers and organizers for the event. Cheering on other riders as they cross the finish is appreciated by everyone.

One of the big keys to your recovery is to behave as you normally would if you just had been out for a fun ride with some of your buddies. In a way that's just what happened. You trained for this event. You tapered for this event. You were ready for this event. In that sense, finishing strongly was what you expected to do. It's not as though you won the lottery or were selected to be on the TV show *Survivor*. So there is no real reason to celebrate as though you did. Take it easy on the beer, don't eat too many plates of barbecue, and go to sleep at the time you normally would. The next day you may be a little bit sore, but if you have the time and feel able, go for a quick ride. Half an hour at an easy pace will do much to reduce your soreness. A long walk or swim will work as well. Don't overdo it, but try to stay active for the next few days.

And enjoy that feeling of accomplishment. You just rode 100 miles on a bicycle!

By the weekend, you should be feeling great and happily leading out the others in your group. And smiling to yourself as you plot your next Century Ride.

Dave's Training Log— Week 15

Date	Sleep/Wt.	Workout	Notes
Mon	8 hrs/168		
Tue	8 hrs/167		
Wed	9 hrs/168	1 hr: moderate pace	Looking forward to this weekend
Thu	8 hrs/168		
Fri	8 hrs/167		
Sat	9 hrs/168		(drove to mountains—took kids to waterfalls)
Sun	6 hrs/167	CENTURY RIDE! 6 hrs: Finished	Long day; lots of riders; felt like a hero at the finish

Total Riding Hours: **7**
Total Miles: **116**

SOURCES

Borg, G.A. "Psychophysical bases of perceived exertion." *Medicine and Science in Sports and Exercise* 14(5) (1982): 377–381.

Burke, Edmund R., PhD, and Ed Pavelka. *The Complete Book of Long-Distance Cycling*. Emmaus, Pennsylvania: Rodale Press Inc., 2000.

California Vehicle Code 2004. www.DMV.CA.gov/pubs.htm

The editors of *Bicycling* magazine. *Long-Distance Cycling*. Emmaus, Pennsylvania: Rodale Press Inc., 1993.

Edwards, Sally. *The Heart Rate Monitor Guidebook*. Adelaide, Australia: Performance Matters Pty Ltd, 1999.

Hurst, Robert. *The Art of Urban Cycling*. Guilford, Connecticut: Globe Pequot Press, 2004.

Jeukendrup, Asker E., PhD. *High Performance Cycling*. Champaign, Illinois: Human Kinetics Publishers Inc., 2002.

Leek, Stephen and Sybil Leek. *The Bicycle—That Curious Invention*. Nashville: Thomas Nelson Inc., 1973.

Yeager, Selene. www.bicycling.com/articles

INDEX

Boldface page references indicate photographs.
<u>Underscored</u> references indicate boxed text.